God

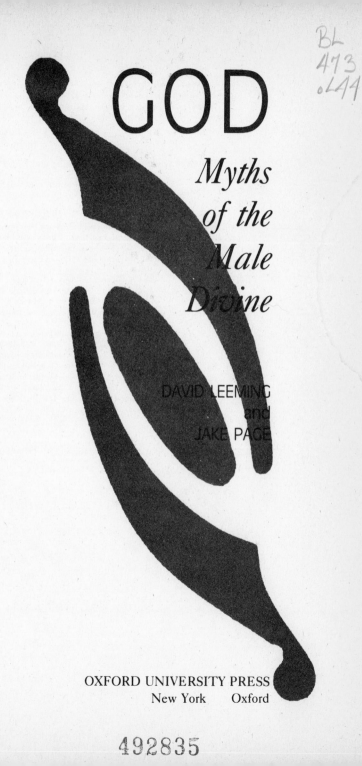

GOD

*Myths
of the
Male
Divine*

DAVID LEEMING
and
JAKE PAGE

OXFORD UNIVERSITY PRESS
New York   Oxford

Oxford University Press

Oxford   New York
Athens   Auckland   Bangkok   Bogota   Bombay   Buenos Aires
Calcutta   Cape Town   Dar es Salaam   Delhi   Florence   Hong Kong
Istanbul   Karachi   Kuala Lumpur   Madras   Madrid   Melbourne
Mexico City   Nairobi   Paris   Singapore   Taipei   Tokyo   Toronto

and associated companies in
Berlin   Ibadan

Copyright © 1996 by David Leeming and Jake Page

First published by Oxford University Press, Inc., 1996.
First issued as an Oxford University Press paperback, 1997

Oxford is a registered trademark of Oxford University Press

Library of Congress Cataloging-in-Publication Data
Leeming, David Adams, 1937–
God : myths of the male divine /
David Leeming and Jake Page.
p.   cm.
Includes bibliographical references and index.
ISBN 0-19-509306-2
ISBN 0-19-511387-X (Pbk.)
1. God—Comparative studies.
2. Gods—Comparative studies.
I. Page, Jake.   II. Title.
BL473.L44   1996   291.2'113—dc20   95-9236

Interior ornaments by Donna Maria Ramirez.

1 2 3 4 5 6 7 8 9 10
Printed in the United States of America

*For
the
grandfathers,
fathers,
uncles,
sons,
grandsons,
brothers,
and
nephews*

Preface

On a day in January, we dedicated ourselves to sit down at separate desks in a house on the edge of a sandy mesa in New Mexico and begin the actual work of producing this book. We had talked, of course, and thought, and schemed, and it seemed evident that the beginning of a biography of God would have to start before human memory—a time that we know from a few eerie artifacts and, perhaps, from the minds of some societies who have been least affected by the tumultuous progress of mankind. And so we talked about The Trickster.

The trickster is a fringy sort of character, a lowlife full of appetites that make the good and faithful a bit nervous. He is also a creator, sometimes *the* creator.

We had talked about the trickster in our world today—he is Sam Spade, a private eye, the antiheroic fellow not quite within the law, who organizes what becomes justice. He is the maverick, who can crash and burn in a private plane or a fast car, or maybe start a whole new industry.

But while we were talking, postponing that moment when we had to *begin*, to act, to create, we heard a rude and slovenly gutteral cry. It was a raven flying over the house. In fact, it was two ravens, and they played in the updrafts brought about by the verticality of the mesa. They did barrel rolls, and looped the loop, and cackled. We have heard that ravens sometimes pester wolves in this way.

The raven is, of course, a notable trickster in the world of many American Indians, eclipsed in acclaim for meddling in

the affairs of god and men only by the coyote, the other notable Indian trickster figure.

And this is what happened. After the ravens flew off to
some nefarious doings, there appeared a coyote, ten feet from
the house we sat in. It is not uncommon to hear coyotes in the
town, but none had ever showed up in the yard before this
day.

So we proceeded into the world of God, hoping that some-
body was smiling on our efforts.

Corrales, N.M.   D. L.
February 1995   J. P.

Acknowledgments

The authors are indebted to several scholars whose work on
mythology has provided significant information and source
material. Works by Roger D. Abrahams, Karen Armstrong,
Anne Baring and Jules Cashford, John Bierhorst, Joseph
Campbell, R. T. Rundle Clark, Kevin Crossley-Holland,
Mircea Eliade, Richard Erdoes and Alfonso Ortiz, Henry
Louis Gates, Jr., Marija Gimbutas, Robert Graves, Samuel
Noah Kramer and John Maier, G. Rachel Levy, Charles Long,
James Mellaart, Wendy Doniger O'Flaherty, Walter Otto,
John Weir Perry, Paul Radin, Barbara Sproul, Hamilton A.
Tyler, Mary Weigle, Diane Wolkstein, and Heinrich Zimmer
have been particularly useful.

Translations of segments of the *Gilgamesh* epic are by
Samuel Noah Kramer and Diane Wolkstein.

All illustrations are drawn by Jake Page, unless otherwise
noted.

Contents

God

Introduction

It is generally accepted that the concept of deity emerged at an early stage of human development. The sophistication of early Stone Age cave paintings and artifacts supports this assumption. Deities would seem to be projections of the species' sense of a significant reality beyond its own immediate understanding and of its attempt, nevertheless, to achieve intellectual and emotional security by relating itself to that reality. The confrontation with deity is the confrontation of humanity with its ultimate boundaries within and outside of itself.

To communicate with this "Great Mystery," humans, naturally enough, have had to make use of the elements of their own experience of existence, as well as artificial means—costumes, masks, dance, art, music, sacrifice, stories, drugs—by which to raise themselves to a "higher" level of perception appropriate to a contemplation of our experience of the "other." The specific shapes applied to the Great Mystery, not surprisingly more often than not, have been based on the highest form of which humans can conceive. To be sure, humans have created deities in animal guise and as various other elements of creation, but almost always with a human-like component. "No man hath ever seen God," but humans have conceived of their deities in their own image, as thinking, talking, creative and procreative gods and goddesses, reflecting their sense of a superiority that rests on an assumption that the human being of all animals is the one who can make creation conscious of itself, whether by projecting experience onto a cave wall, a musical work, a painting, or the concept of deity itself.

Once humans conceive of divinity in their own image they must see deities as male and female—gods and goddesses—in spite of the fact that to attribute gender to Supreme Beings is to limit them by tying them to our own reproductive cycles and, therefore, to our own death-defined experience. Very few religions or mythologies—one group's religion is another's mythology—perceive a genderless deity. While many see their Supreme Beings as immortal, as powers beyond the confines of nature, almost all cultures contradict that understanding—at least at the metaphorical level—by, in effect, giving them primary sexual characteristics.

In *Goddess: Myths of the Female Divine*, to which this book is a sequel, we traced the development of the female metaphor for deity from Paleolithic times to the present. We now approach the question of the male metaphor. As the first book was the "biography" of the goddess archetype, this sequel is the biography of the god archetype, *god* being the term we commonly apply to the many masks in which the male form of deity has emerged into human consciousness over the centuries. An *archetype*, in the sense in which we use the term, is a universal tendency of the human psyche that takes particular but related personal and cultural forms in the dreams, myths, rituals, and arts of the species.

By studying the female or male metaphor for the Great Mystery in a given culture we can learn a great deal about that culture's particular experience of reality and something about its experience of and reaction to its sense of the feminine or masculine aspects of its being. It follows that as we watch the development of the goddess or god archetypes through history, we can see something of the human species' experience of and reaction to *its* sense of the feminine and masculine aspects of *its* being.

Having said this, it is important to remind ourselves, that whether in the particular cultural context or the larger universal one, we can only perceive the archetype—in this case the god archetype—indirectly in the many forms it takes: rituals, works of art, dreams, and myths. We must remember, too, that our biography cannot be purely linear. It is true that there is a general movement historically from a god who is clearly subservient and inferior to the Great Goddess of the Paleolithic and Neolithic ages to the Abrahamic-type dominant male deity who comes to power later. But the details of the history are less simple. At any given time, one group might honor a supreme goddess and a secondary god while another culture attaches itself to a monotheistic male figure. The Abrahamic "God," after all, is still today "only a myth" to the Okanagan believer in the Mother Creator as well as to the atheist or agnostic crossing Fifth Avenue.

It needs to be said, too, that our "biography" is not strictly chronological in terms of the individual "masks of God" or the murkier universal shadow figure that they reveal. That is, the Paleolithic gods and the archetypal being they point to were not children, and the later Christian god, for instance, is not only a "grown up." As the goddess archetype could take form as crone, woman, and maiden at any given time, the god archetype can also be at once the ancient one, the god of the ruling pantheon, and the Divine Child.

We are led now to the whole question of the term *god*. In Western culture the term has been appropriated by the great monotheistic religions as the name "God," and all of us in the West—believers, agnostics, and atheists—live in the presence of that name. In searching for the essence of the god archetype, however, we are not searching for "God." We are not suggesting, as did the scholar Wilhelm Schmidt in his *Origin of the Idea of God* in 1912, that humans believed in a form of "God" before they fell into polytheism. This is decidedly not an attempt to find the Judeo-Christian God in all myths and religions. Our approach will suggest that the Judeo-Christian-Islamic "God" is but one mask—albeit a sophisticated and complex one—of a reality that lies behind all the many gods that the human mind has described in its myths and religions. There is no attempt here to prove that monotheisism is a higher form of religion than polytheism or that Yahweh, God, or Allah are names for truth while Siva and Osiris are "mere myths." At its most basic level, the human experience of religion cannot be said to be monotheistic, except in a highly philosophical and rationalized sense. Nor can it be called essentially polytheistic, except in an absurdly literal sense. What is important is the pervasive human experience or sense of a divine reality in the universe and our need as a species to understand it.

We are looking for the Great Mystery behind not only the mask called Allah (from *al-illah* meaning "the god"), but behind the one called Nnui ("He who is Everywhere") by the Bamun people of Cameroon, the one called Siva ("the Auspicious One") by Hindus, and the one called the "horned God" by practitioners of Wicca. Inevitably we are led to obvious recognitions such as the connection between the Christian Father-Creator/Christ-Redeemer/Holy Spirit–Sanctifier and the Hindu Brahma-Creator/Visnu-Preserver/Siva-Yogi-Destroyer trinities, in both of which the specific elements of the triads are not each other but are all in some mysterious way "God" and "Brahman." And we will find less obvious connections as well. The point is, the God of our biography has many faces, many moods, many ways of being. He can be kind, all-knowing, beneficent, just, cruel, a philanderer, a loving or jealous father and husband, a trickster, an oppressor of the weak and of women, a suppressor of Goddess, a Creator.

As Goddess contains all the possibilities of the feminine, God contains those of the masculine. It is certainly true that there are aspects of what might be called the Hermes type or the Zeus type or the Coyote type in most men and that some are more one type than the other. But it must also be said that God does not belong only to men any more than Goddess does to women. Women tend to identify with Goddess imagery whereas men tend to identify with God imagery, but God and Goddess are emanations of us all and are contained within us all. Persephone is the sexually oppressed woman, but she is also the possibility of rebirth and growth for men and women. Apollo speaks to the rationality that men like to associate with themselves as opposed to women, whom they have tended to depict as at best intuitive or at worst hysterical, but he also speaks with his motto ("Know thyself") to the inner drive for balance and wholeness to which we all strive.

The God behind the many cultural embodiments collected here has an existence that transcends those forms and speaks to a central aspect of our collective sense of identity. His biography, along with that of Goddess, is a record of what we humans believe ourselves to be at the deepest level.

I

The Birth of the Archetype: Trickster/Shaman/ Animal Master

Rock painting of the "Sorcerer," a shaman-trickster god, Les Trois Frères Cave (France, ca. 14,000 B.C.E.). (After H. Breuil)

God was born sometime in the Paleolithic Age, the Old Stone Age, which corresponds historically to the geological ice age. There are indications of religious cults in altars and burial sites that date back to the time of Neanderthal Man (*Homo sapiens neanderthalis*), that is, as early as the Middle Paleolithic (ca. 75,000 B.C.E.). But the first clear pictures we have of male deity are on the walls of the great caves of Cro-Magnon Man (*Homo sapiens sapiens*) in Europe, Africa, and Asia during the early part of the Upper Paleolithic (30,000–10,000 B.C.E.) period. The Upper Paleolithic was marked by the development of bladed stone tools, by some cave dwelling, by hunting and gathering and later fishing, and by the emergence of art in the form of sculpture and painting.

In most of the world this was an age in which the damp dark caves with their multitude of vulva depictions were perhaps representational precincts of a life-bearing Goddess. The paintings and carvings that represent this female figure certainly greatly outnumber those that depict the male. But there is a sufficient number of paintings and engravings to support the assumption of a Paleolithic sense of sacredness associated with the male as well. The depictions are usually of ithyphallic, sometimes bird-masked, sometimes bearded, men. Frequently there are animals and details such as animal droppings in the drawings, and animal–men combinations.

There is, of course, no direct access to the meanings of these figures or to the myths of this preliterate period. What we can determine of the nature of the Paleolithic myths of God must come from a blending together of the cave art and our knowledge of the myths and rituals of peoples who have brought what might be called a Paleolithic lifestyle into the post-Paleolithic ages. It is primarily to the hunter-gatherer societies of Africa and North America that we must look for

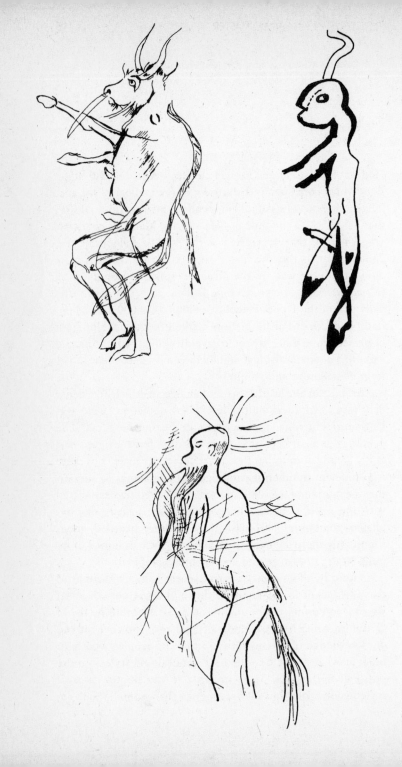

Cave paintings and engravings (ca. 17,000–13,000 B.C.E.): bison-man, Les Trois Frères Cave (France); bird-man, La Pileta Cave (Spain); bearded man, Espélugues Cave (France); ritual hunt with droppings, Lascaux Cave (France). (After Marija Gimbutas)

indications of the nature of Paleolithic mythology and of the birth of the god archetype.

The most famous of the Paleolithic cave paintings is the so-called Sorcerer (ca. 14,000 B.C.E.) of what many have called the "Sistine Chapel of the Paleolithic Age," the cave of Les Trois Frères at Lascaux in the French Pyrenees.

The combination of animal characteristics with those of the human—the antlered (horned) but bearded face, the dancing human legs, with the torso placed in the four-legged animal position, parallel to the ground, the emphasized human genitals located in a feline position under a bushy tail—all suggest the shaman as we know him in later Paleolithic-type cultures.

The shaman is a possessor of magic powers, which are

dangerous but useful. He is one to be avoided unless needed and is, by definition, a loner. One of his jobs is to apply his powers to the hunting of animals so that the group might have sufficient provisions. Dressed in his animal costume, the sorcerer-shaman relates himself to the animals he is stalking; he represents the "animal master" who convinces the animals to give themselves to the people. So the hunt becomes a ritual sacrifice rather than an act of murder, and the sacrificed animal is the willing victim and the ancestor of those later man-gods who die that their people might prosper. Approached properly, the hunt will bring about not the decimation of the animals but their constant renewal. This renewal is perhaps suggested by the prominent phallus of the cave sorcerer.

The following is a shamanic myth told by the Cherokee Indians.

Bear Man

A man trekked up into the mountains bent on killing a bear. Eventually he spotted one and shot it with an arrow from his bow. The bear spun around and ran noisily into the sun-dappled forest, crashing through the underbrush. The hunter pursued, loosing arrow after arrow at the bear, but the wounded bear simply would not fall.

Finally, the bear stopped and pulled the hunter's arrows from its body and held them out to the man.

"There's no use shooting these arrows at me," the bear said. "You cannot kill me." The hunter then realized that this was a medicine bear, protected by magic. "Come to my house," the bear said. "We can live together."

The hunter immediately feared for his life, but the bear knew his thoughts. "No, no," it said. "I won't hurt you." The hunter next wondered to himself what he would eat if he lived with this magical bear. And the bear said: "There will be plenty to eat."

So the hunter followed along until they came to a hole in the side of the mountain.

"This isn't where I live, but there will be a council here, and we should attend it to see what they do."

Inside, the hole widened out into a vast cave with houses ringing it. Many bears had assembled there already—old and young bears, bears of all colors—and the chief of all the bears was a huge white one.

The hunter and his companion slipped into a corner to wait for the council to begin, but the bears began sniffing the air and complaining of a bad smell. Hearing this, the bear chief said: "Don't make rude comments. It is only a stranger who has joined us. Leave him alone."

The council meeting concerned the growing scarcity of food in the mountains, but some bears had found a new feeding ground where the chestnuts and acorns were plentiful, so the bears held a dance of celebration and thanks. Afterward, the bears filed out of the cave and went home. The hunter and his companion bear left as well, and eventually came to another hole, the bear's home, and went in.

Knowing the hunter was hungry, the bear rubbed his stomach and his paws filled up with food—huckleberries, blackberries, and acorns—enough for the hunter and the bear to live through the cold sleep of winter when time stands still. As the winter wore on, the man grew long hair on his body, like that of the bear, and learned the ways of bears.

Spring came and the earth began to warm, and the bear said: "Your people down below, they are getting ready to come into the mountains for a big hunt. They will find this cave and kill me. They will take away my clothes and cut me into pieces. No, No, they will not kill you. They will take you home with them. Do not be fearful."

And soon, when the earth was a little warmer, the bear said: "This is the day they come. Their dogs, the split-noses, will find me, and the men will drag me out and skin me and cut me up. You must cover up my blood with leaves and go with them. But when they are taking me away, look back and you will see something."

Sure enough, dogs approached and barked, the men shot
arrows into the cave, killing the bear, and they dragged him
outside, skinned him and quartered him. Then they looked
back in the cave, thinking they saw another bear. The hunter
quivered in fear, but the men realized that, under the long
bear-like fur, it was the hunter who had disappeared a year
earlier. They invited him to come home with them.

Before leaving, the hunter piled leaves over the bloody
spot where his bear companion had been skinned and butch-
ered. Sadly, he set off after the men but paused and turned
around. And from under the leaves the bear rose up on his
hind legs and shook his great shoulders. Then he dropped to
the ground and disappeared into the warming forest.

In this myth we find several aspects of the shamanic experience. It is a story of a young man's calling and his initiation
into what we can see are shamanic mysteries associated with
the relationship between man and animal. The shamanic aspect resides in the animal master himself, the Great Bear, who
can read minds and provide food by the mere rubbing of his
belly, and who can transcend death. These characteristics
would suggest that he is also a version of God, the Animal God
as master shaman. The young man he takes into his cave for a
season is the shaman apprentice, the initiate who will take the
"mysteries" he has learned back to his people, who will wear
the shamanic animal fur grown during his time with the master, and who will perform the regenerative rituals taught him.

The "Sorcerer" of Trois Frères is such a figure, and his
pronounced phallus has ithyphallic descendants in the satyrs
and centaurs and phallus-bearing herm statues familiar to students of Greek culture and mythology and in the phallic depictions of the West African gods who contain the secrets of
fecundity and are guardians of crossroads. By the time of the
cave painting the phallus had achieved a status equivalent to
the vulva as a symbol of regenerative power.

We can imagine the Trois Frères sorcerer dressed in his

Bear shaman. (After George Catlin)

costume doing other things that shamans do, not only providing the boon of food but curing the sick and assuring individual and general fertility by penetrating the earth (perhaps
by way of the mysterious goddess caves) and entering the
spirit world to intercede for the ordinary people above.
Shamans take such journeys, and it is said that some do not
come back. Some lose bones and some die. The noninitiate
may well explain such failures by falls and heart attacks

brought on by the excitement of the ritual or by drug-induced seizures, but the initiate believes that the shaman's spirit journey is a real and dangerous one. The shaman has descendants in the heroes who journey to the underworld in the myths of the Neolithic (New Stone Age [ca. 7000–2000 B.C.E.] and into the present age in parts of the world).

This is the initiatory dream of a Siberian Samoyed shaman, which amply illustrates the shaman spirit journey.

Samoyed Shaman Dream

Call him Tavgytsy. The illness was upon him and for three days he lay unconscious, so near death that by the end of the third day his people had concluded that the burial ceremonies should commence.

But Tavgytsy was not dead. Instead he had been carried into the middle of the sea where a voice called out to him. It was the voice of the Sickness, telling him that he would receive from the Deities of the Water a great gift and a name. He would be Diver, the shaman. And the sea around him trembled and roiled.

Tavgytsy struggled out of the sea and a mountain rose before him, which he climbed, finding at the summit a naked woman—the Lady of the Water—on whose undulating breast he suckled hungrily.

"You are my child," soothed the Lady of the Water, "so I let you suckle at my breast. For many hardships will befall you and you will be wearied to the very bone."

Her husband then appeared, the Lord of the Underworld, along with an ermine and a mouse who were to be Tavgytsy's guides for the journey on which, in an instant, he found himself: on another high place, standing before seven tents each with its roof torn and open to the elements. Compelled to enter, he found the first tent filled with the denizens of the underworld and sickness who received him into their midst by tearing the heart from his chest and throwing it gleefully into a pot. Under the same compulsion, he left and visited the remaining six tents, where he was regaled by the Lord of Madness and the lords of all other human disorders, learning at first hand the wiles and ways of the host of diseases that wreak torment on humankind.

The ermine and the mouse beckoned him on to the Land of the Shamanesses who set about fondling his throat, weaving magic with his voice, until he found to his amazement that he could sing. And singing still, he was transported to an island in the middle of a sea, itself one of nine seas that shimmered to the horizon. In the middle of the island where he found himself, a slender birch tree, silvery white with black tongue marks, rose toward the heavens. This, Tavgytsy knew without guidance, was the Tree of the Lord of the Earth. Around its glistening trunk in the damp earth grew nine herbs, the ancestors of all the world's plants, and all around him, offshore, birds of all kinds along with their young bobbed on the surface of the manifold seas.

To each of these seas, Tavgytsy went—to the salty ones, to those that were too hot to wade into, and then returned to the slender birch growing above the parental plants. It became clear to him how the herbs could heal the sicknesses that tormented humanity. High in the tree's branches above, he saw men—men of the many tribes and nations—and heard their voices.

Was it *their* voices?

He heard the words: You shall have a drum made from the branches of this tree. And the voice, now a single voice, that of the Lord of the Tree, instructed him to make a drum from a three-forked branch of the tree, and said: "I am the Tree that gives all life to men." And he could see now the arts of the healer, the shaman: they were inscribing themselves in his mind as clearly as the pattern of the birch's bark.

He was now among the seven stones which spoke to him, telling him how they could help men, how they also held down the earth with their weight lest it be carried off in the wind. From there, his guides led him to a bright cave with walls of mirrors and a fire-like core. Two naked women with the pelts of reindeer gave him, each, a hair from their body

Eskimo shaman. (After Jessie Oonark)

and gave birth to awkward reindeer young themselves. These animals, which would be food and succor to the people of the forest, unfolded their spindly legs, arose, and went forth from the cave.

Tavgytsy also went forth, finding yet another cave on yet another mountain, this one rising from a trackless desert and silhouetted by an enormous fire in the cave's center, was a naked man tending a caldron half as big as the earth itself.

Before Tavgytsy could think beyond his own death, the naked man seized him, lopped off his head, sliced his body into pieces and threw these gory gobbets into the cauldron where they boiled for three years. After this eternity, the man of the fire molded a new head for Tavgytsy and taught it to read the words that appear both outside and inside it. He put new flesh on the parboiled bones. He placed new eyes in the head, eyes that see things bodily eyes cannot, and pierced its ears with knowledge.

And Tavgytsy awoke in his yurt among his family and his

people. He was Diver now. Whenever he needed to, he could return to the dire and dangerous caves of his journey, and he could sing and drum and heal mankind.

As long as he lived, he could do all this without ever becoming tired.

Still another duty of the shaman as we know him is to preserve the rituals and the sacred traditions of the group. To this day, Navajo shamans or medicine men memorize the sacred chant-ceremonies for use in the constant struggle to preserve harmony within the individual, the clan, and the tribe.

In a Navajo healing ceremony, or "sing," called the Red Antway, numerous songs are sung over the patient during four days, and sometimes as many as nine. This one (paraphrased here from the Horned Toad Songs) begins after an emetic has boiled and cooled. The song continues—in all, nine songs that are basically the same except for the key words—as the patient drinks the emetic and vomits through a small hoop. First, the medicine man puts the emetic in the proper ceremonial place.

Navajo Shaman Chant

Truly it is terrifying. He has placed it.
Truly it is terrifying. He has placed it.
The sun holds it up. He has placed it.
Holy Young Man has placed it.
And the Swallow People's arrowshaft. Now he has placed it.
To your toes, the evils begin to move.
To your toes, they move out.
Utterly away from you they begin to move; utterly away from you they follow each other, utterly away from you they float.

He will kill the evil thing's witchery, so he has placed it.
It is terrifying. He has placed it.
Now Holy Young Woman has placed it down.
She holds up the moon. She has placed it.
She has placed the powerful Swallows' arrowhead.
The evils begin moving to the tip of your mouth; to the tip of your mouth they move out.
Utterly away from you, they begin to move out; utterly away from you, they follow each other; utterly away from you, they float out.
He will kill the evil thing's witchery, so he has placed it.
It is terrifying. He has placed it.

The chant goes repetitively on through the various steps: after (1) he "has placed it," (2) it proceeds into your interior, (3) the evil within is frightened, (4) it leaves your interior, (5) he is driving it out, (6) it turns away from you, (7) the evil turns upon him, (8) he kills it, (9) he has killed it.

Shamanic functions have tended to be assimilated into the more orderly priestly arrangements of planting cultures such as the ones that began to develop in the Fertile Crescent (present-day Iraq) and elsewhere in the Neolithic. By definition, shamans with their powerful magic are to be feared. Navajos today still fear the medicine man, knowing that his shamanic powers could all too easily be applied to the dark arts of witchcraft. The stalking, dancing, but uncontrollable outsider shaman of the hunters, and to some extent of the herders, will become the horned, costumed kachina of particular animal clans of tribes like the Hopi, Zuni, and Rio Grande Pueblo people. These people depend on the kachina, after they emerge from the village kivas (the priestly remnant of the old maternal caves, where the men of the group perform their sacred rituals and arts), to intercede for rain with the spirit world that they represent and somehow magically become.

The question of the shaman becoming the god is one that has been addressed by many scholars. The Abbe Breuil, Joseph Campbell, and Marija Gimbutas have all suggested,

Billy Yellow, Navajo shaman. (Photograph by Susanne Page)

A kachina emerges from a kiva.

for instance, that the Trois Frères sorcerer is in reality a "god." In him, they say, the master shaman has indeed become the master of animals. At the very least, by donning the sacred animal costumes, he has taken on divine power the way a kachina-masked Hopi or a vested Catholic priest does. In his costume he is, for the time of his ritual, the god incarnate.

The connection between the cave paintings and what we know of shamanic traditions provides a crucial clue to the nature of the actual mythology of the Paleolithic period. When we look at the Trois Frères shaman-god and think of the legend of the Cherokee Bear Man and the initiatory dream of the Samoyed shaman, we find ourselves inevitably confronted by a figure who is as troubling as he is pervasive in world mythology, especially in the mythologies of the hunter-gatherers of Africa and North America. This figure is the trickster, a significant mask of God and in all probability his earliest. Indeed, Joseph Campbell has called the trickster probably "the chief mythological character of the Paleolithic world of story" (*Masks: Primitive Mythology*, 273), and it seems likely that trickster mythology is the mythology behind the institution of shamanism.

The trickster, like the sorcerer of Trois Frères, is a phallic figure. Whether the North American Coyote, Iktome (Inktomi, Ictinike, Spider), Raven, or the African Anansi (Ananse, Spider), he is sexually overactive, irresponsible, and amoral. But it is that very phallicism that signifies his essential creativity, and the trickster is almost always either an assistant to the creator or the creator himself. Like the shaman, he contains the sacred magic and can transcend human limitations; he can transform himself or other things at will; he can move between the worlds and can even bring life out of death. Yet the trickster is thoroughly human, even when wearing his animal "mask." He is obsessed by human desires for food and sex and he is often the butt of his own tricks, and even in his creative acts he is often crude and "immature." He is obsessed by defecation and by body parts, reminding us once again of those Paleolithic cave paintings with their vulvas, exaggerated phalluses, and frequent depictions of animal droppings.

It can reasonably be suggested that the trickster, whom Carl Jung saw as the representation of a preconscious human state, became "civilized" in the great-god culture heroes of the late Neolithic and post-Neolithic periods, sacrificial victims who overcome death and travel to the other world for the good of all.

What follows is a small collection of myths that will illustrate characteristics of the trickster aspect of the God archetype as developed in various parts of the world.

The Polynesian people tell many versions of the story of Maui, the trickster who stole the wife of the Great Eel Te Tuna ("The Penis"). Many of the trickster elements are here: the Animal God, the phallicism, the amorality, the creativeness, the transformations, the transcending of human boundaries.

Maui

Now, in the land under the sea lived the Monster Eel, known as Te Tuna which means "The Penis." In the frigid torpor of his land, he was slow in motion, slow to respond, a fact that was not lost on his beautiful consort, Hina. So, on the pretext of setting out to look for food for the two of them, Hina went off one day seeking lovers to match her passion.

She soon arrived at the distant land of the Male-Principle Clan and called out her intentions, announcing that she had left the disappointing and insipid Te Tuna, and sought an eel-shaped rod of love.

"I am the dark and shameless pubic patch seeking the release of desire," she said. "I have come a long way for this, so let your staffs rise up tumescent and plunge into love's consummation."

"Oh, no," shouted the men of the clan. "Te Tuna would kill us if we did. There is the road—keep going."

So Hina journeyed on, her loins aflame, and was rebuffed twice more until she came to the land of the Maui Clan, the wonder-workers, and repeated her challenging call. Now, Maui himself had fished up the very islands from the sea, had slowed down the sun in its passage, and lifted the sky off the earth to make room for people to live. He had stolen fire for his mother to use in her kitchen, and she was always on the lookout for ways to reward his heroic acts. So when she saw Hina approaching, she told Maui to bestir himself and take the beautiful stranger for his own.

Needing no further prompting, Maui claimed Hina and they lived together in exquisite passion there for many days. But then people realized this was Te Tuna's wife sporting in their midst and went to tell the Monster Eel. Te Tuna merely shrugged torpidly saying that Maui could have her. But people continued to gossip to him about Hina until, finally, he got angry.

"What is this Maui like," he asked contemptuously, "this mere man?"

"He's not very big," the gossips said, "and the end of his penis is lopsided."

"Well, let him get a look at this," Te Tuna said, waving the soiled loincloth that hung between his legs, "and he will fly away."

The people reported to Maui that Te Tuna was coming for revenge and Maui, unconcerned, asked what sort of creature Te Tuna was. An enormous monster, they replied.

"Is he sturdy, strong as an upright tree?" Maui asked, and the gossips explained that he was like a leaning tree, ever bent. But they remained fearful, since this was the first time anyone could remember when someone had stolen the wife of another. "We will all be killed," they moaned, but Maui told them not to worry.

Sure enough, the skies soon darkened, lightning tore at the heavens and thunder boomed across the surface of the earth. Te Tuna, the Penis, approached in fury, accompanied by four other monsters. He stripped off his disgusting loincloth and held it high, and as he did so, the sea surged high and a towering wall of water surged toward the land. The people recoiled in panic, but Maui's mother shouted to her son: "Quick! Show him yours!"

So Maui loosed his lopsided penis and raised it against the surging waters. The wave subsided, leaving the monsters high and dry on a reef, and Maui leapt on them and dispatched them—all but Te Tuna, whom he spared. Instead, he invited the Monster Eel to share his house.

There was a period of harmony but, of course, it could not last. One day, Te Tuna said a duel was necessary, the winner to take Hina exclusively for himself. First, he said, there must be a contest in which each entered the body of the other. After that, he said, "I'll kill you and take Hina home to my land beneath the sea." Again, Maui shrugged, and told Te Tuna to go first.

So chanting a song, and swinging and swaying his head, the Monster Eel grew smaller and smaller and disappeared into Maui's body, where he intended to stay for good, thus enjoying Hina's charms from within. But soon Maui ejected him, and singing his own song, shrank and entered Te Tuna, tearing apart the monster's very flesh and sinew and killing him.

Stepping lightly out, Maui lopped off the monster's head and, at his mother's suggestion, planted it near the corner of his house. Peace and love-making resumed in the land of the wonder-workers, and one afternoon Maui noticed a green shoot growing from the place where Te Tuna's head had been buried.

Maui's mother explained that this was a tree that would bear a coconut with a sea-green husk and told her son to take care of it. When the tree grew and its fruit ripened, Maui plucked it. The coconut's meat was eaten by all, and everyone danced to celebrate how Maui had killed the Monster Eel and turned his head into food.

And that is how the people of this world came to have the coconut to eat.

In the Krishna lore of India, we find a Hindu trickster in the greatest of Visnu's incarnations, the Lord Krishna, for some the embodiment of godhead itself. This myth is from the *Bhagavata Purana*.

Krishna (I)

When Visnu—for the sport of it—took up residence in a human form, it was as a little boy who was known as Krishna. And when Krishna played the games of children with his companions, it was a source of great delight to the mothers of the village. But they soon realized that, when he thought no one was looking, Krishna would play especially mischievous pranks.

He would untie the calves, steal curds and milk, give food to the monkeys, even make the other children cry. He would poke holes in the bottom of pots holding milk, adorn himself with jewels he took—he even snuck into peoples' houses and peed on their clean floors. The women took it upon themselves to report all this to Krishna's mother one day, but instead of scolding him, she looked into his beautiful face with its innocent dark eyes and laughed.

But one day, the other women told her that her son Krishna had eaten dirt from the ground. She took him by the hand and scolded him, and he said, "Mother, I haven't eaten dirt. They all lie. Look in my mouth and see for yourself."

Krishna opened his mouth and his mother looked inside. There she saw mountains, islands, seas. She saw the winds, lightning, the moon, the stars. She saw the elements, the strands of matter, and life, time, action, hope—the entire universe appeared before her in the boy's gaping mouth, and she was stunned. Is this, she wondered, a delusion, or a god-wrought dream? Is my little son a god in whom the unfathomable universe is present? Through this god, am I given the illusion that I exist, that this is my son?

As she took her little son on her lap in a wave of maternal love, her memory of this vision disappeared, replaced only by a deepened love for her son and the knowledge that the great god Visnu was indeed present in her little boy.

As Krishna grew to manhood, his heroic exploits became known far and wide and he gained the reputation of lord of all masters of yoga. In his own village, the girls all yearned to have him as husband, and one winter they all took a vow to the goddess Katyayani, swearing to worship her so that Krishna would be theirs. They repeated this vow for a month, rising at dawn to bathe together in the Kalindi River and sing of Krishna.

One day, they had left their clothes on the riverbank, as usual, and were playing and diving in the water like river otters, joyfully singing about their yearnings to be joined with Krishna. And who should arrive on the riverbank that day among a group of boys his age but Krishna, who laughed as he gathered up the girls' clothes and climbed up a Nipa tree.

From high in the branches he called out that he had come to grant them the goal they sought in their vows to the goddess.

"Let each of you slim-waisted beauties come here and fetch your clothes," he said. "These boys here are my witness: I never lie."

Hearing this, the girls ducked down, red-faced, up to their necks in the water, and giggled among one another, embarrassed but at the same time overcome with love. There in the tree was the object of their fondest desire—but with their very clothes. Flustered, they stayed in the water, shivering in the cold.

"This is a wicked trick," they said. "Give us our clothes first, and we will be your slaves and do whatever you command. But you must give us our clothes, or else we will tell your father."

A great smile shined from Krishna's dark and handsome face. "If you are my slaves," he said, "then I command you to come here and get your clothes."

So the girls emerged from the icy waters, shivering, and approached the tree with hands covering their dark crotches. The sight of their nakedness, and their bashful gesture, pleased Krishna greatly, but he slung their clothes over his shoulder and said: "By swimming naked in the water while under a vow, you have insulted the divinity. To atone for this, you must fold your hands over your head, bow low, and then come to take your clothes."

Since this command had come from the lord of the masters of yoga, and the very object of their hearts' desire, they obeyed, and the sight pleased Krishna even further.

Though they had been deceived and toyed with, the girls clustered around Krishna, happy to be close to him, and as they donned their clothes, he told them they should return to the village where they would henceforth enjoy their nights with him.

The great trickster of northern Europeans is Loki. Like all other tricksters, he is selfish, dangerous, and amoral. He is a transformer, who can take any form, animal or human, male or female. He is funny and he is crude. Yet, like so many tricksters, he provides humanity with certain boons, such as fire and light. He is, above all, a creator.

Loki

They say that you can hear Loki beating his children in the crackling of a fire on the hearth. They say that Loki was none other than Satan stalking the earth, and that he murdered Baldr, the beloved son of Odin, but none of that may ring true. . . .

To be sure, he was greedy, selfish, dangerous. He knew the foibles of all the gods and goddesses; indeed, he was himself the foible of many a goddess, having fast-talked his way into their beds. He was a handsome devil, a thief (there's no denying that), and he could be good company.

On one occasion, it was Loki's wiles that rescued Thor

(not to mention his wife, Freya) from a terrible humiliation. Thor, it seems, woke up one morning to find his precious hammer missing. He mentioned this to Loki who told him that it must have been taken by a giant, and he offered to go forth himself to find it.

In due course, he returned to Asgard, the home of the Aesir, with the news that a giant named Thrym had stolen the hammer, buried it deep in the earth, and would return it only if Freya would be given to him as his wife. This threw the entire assemblage of the Aesir, including Thor, into consternation and, not knowing what to do, they suggested to Freya that it might after all be best if she would . . . well, Freya flew into an indignant fury so great that her neck swelled up and burst her golden necklace.

And that gave Loki an idea. He snatched up the necklace and told Thor to dress up in Freya's bridal clothes. Then he put her necklace around his neck, and the two of them went to pay a visit on Thrym. Thrym was filled with desire when he saw his "bride" and set out a great feast which Thor (in disguise) wolfed down in a most unladylike fashion. Thrym was amazed, but Loki explained that his "bride" had fasted for eight days in anticipation of pleasuring the giant. Then Thrym lifted her veil to kiss her and was startled at her ruddy skin and the fire in her eyes. Loki quickly explained that she had been unable to sleep those same eight days, so feverish had she been for Thrym's lusty attentions.

So Thrym sent for the hammer which, as was custom, he placed on his bride's lap by way of consecrating their union. His bride erupted with a great laugh, picked up the hammer and struck Thrym dead, along with his entire company. And so Thor got his hammer back.

Oh, Loki was fast on his feet. One time he lost a wager by which his head belonged to the dwarf, Brokk, and the slow-witted Brokk announced his intention to claim his prize by separating it from Loki's body.

"My dear Brokk," Loki said, "it is quite true that you have every right to my head. It is yours, and you may take it. *But*," he went on, "nothing, you will recall, was said in our wager about my neck."

The dwarf blinked.

"In taking my head," Loki explained, "you may not take even the slightest shred of my neck."

The dwarf again blinked, his unfertile mind outpaced, and while he puzzled over this, Loki slipped away.

On another occasion, Loki was out wandering with Odin and another god and, famished, they stopped to roast an ox. An eagle settled into a nearby tree and cast a spell which kept the meat from cooking. He said he would lift the spell if the three Aesir would let him eat with them. They acceded, and the eagle settled in, taking all the best cuts of meat. Always quick to anger, Loki thrashed the eagle with a rod.

At this, the eagle flew off, with the rod magically stuck to his body and with Loki magically stuck to the rod. Loki bounced across the ground, bruised and cut, and never one to suffer physical hurt for long, he begged for mercy.

The eagle, who was in fact a giant named Thjazi, said that Loki could have his freedom on the condition that he deliver in his stead the luscious goddess Idun . . . and her apples. These were miraculous apples which kept all the Aesir from growing old. Without a thought for his fellows, Loki swore he would comply.

Back at Asgard, he approached the voluptuous Idun who carried with her, as always, her basket of apples, and he said, "My dear Idun, most sagacious of the goddesses, why don't you come with me for a stroll in the forest. I have something to show you. Something nobody else has ever seen."

"Not on your life," Idun said, for while she was not all that sagacious, she knew Loki's reputation. "And anyway, there are many here who have indeed seen that thing."

"No, no," Loki protested, laughing ingratiatingly. "I came across some apples in the forest, apples even more beautiful than those with which you adorn yourself and so generously share with the Aesir." Idun was soon persuaded, her curiosity piqued, and the two set out into the forest.

Once they were among the trees, Thjazi leapt upon the goddess—as had been arranged—and dragged her off to his home while Loki slipped back into Asgard, free again.

Not long afterward, the Aesir noticed Idun's absence and

wondered where she might be. And then, Idun's apples being absent as well, they began to notice on each other the unmistakable ravages of age. They flew into a rage, blaming Loki for this, and threatened him with dismemberment and death until he agreed to bring the goddess and her apples back.

Changing himself into a hawk, he flew into the kingdom of the giants and alit near Thjazi's home. Finding Idun mourning her lost freedom and her fate at the hands of the gross and callous giant, Loki changed her into a nut and carried her back to Asgard.

In such ways did Loki torment the Aesir until the time came for them to vanish from the affairs of mankind. But these rumors . . . that it was Loki who arranged their disappearance . . . who could believe such a thing?

Hermes is the Greek trickster. Born a thief and a liar, he is also a phallic god; his phallus often was superimposed onto the sacred *herms*, which marked boundaries and guarded doorways in ancient Greece. He was thus a source of fertility. He was also the shaman-like conveyor of souls to the other world, literally a penetrator of the earth womb-tomb.

Hermes

Before most boy-children have learned to walk, Hermes had to be hauled up before Zeus for disciplinary action. One of Zeus's countless bastard children, sired in this instance on Maia, the daughter of Atlas, Hermes was surely a precocious little thief.

Barely had he been born, high atop Mount Cyllene, before he growth-spurted into a little boy and slipped off to find adventure. Before long he came across a herd of fine cattle, tended by Apollo (his half-brother, though he may not have known that at the time), and he resolved to rustle the cows. Lest Apollo track his herd, Hermes made each cow a set of shoes from bark and grass and, in the dead of night, led them off.

When Apollo awoke shining, he was baffled by his herd's disappearance without the trace of a hoofmark. He searched high and low, and finally in exasperation was forced to offer a reward. A group of satyrs led by Silenus, a somewhat over-weight drunk with the ears of a horse, took up the challenge and fanned out far and wide, hoping to win the bounty. In Arcadia, a small band of them heard some eerily unfamiliar music issuing from a cave.

They were met at the cave entrance by a nymph who said that a recently born child had invented an astounding thing: a music toy made from a tortoise shell and cow gut. Noting some cow hides stretched near the entrance, one of the satyrs asked with wine-inspired canniness where the child had got the cow gut, and the nymph huffily asked if the ugly little satyr was accusing an infant child of theft.

Before long, the satyr and the nymph were scream-ing epithets and accusations at each other and the child's mother—Maia herself—woke up in the cave, asking what the fuss was all about. At the moment when Maia pointed to the "sleeping" boy child wrapped in swaddling and called the charge ridiculous, Apollo arrived and recognized the cow hides as his own.

So Apollo snatched Hermes up and hauled him off to Olympus, asking Zeus to judge the matter. Eventually, Hermes confessed to the crime, saying he had slaughtered only two cows from the herd, cutting them up into twelve portions as a sacrifice to the twelve gods.

"Twelve gods?" Apollo asked. "Twelve? Who is the twelfth?"

And Hermes said modestly, "Me." Zeus was greatly amused and in this way Hermes not only arranged for his own inclusion in the highest pantheon of Olympus, but by way of saving his own skin invented the idea of animal sacrifice.

Then Hermes produced the tortoise shell-lyre he had in-vented, sang a song of praise to Apollo's greatness, and traded the lyre to Apollo in return for the cows. Everyone was happy, and Zeus, still amused at the sassiness of this sproutling of his, admonished him to be more respectful of the property of others and not to tell outright falsehoods. Zeus went on to remark that he found Hermes to be a most ingenious godling.

So Hermes offered to be the great god's herald and not to tell lies, though he said he would not always tell the whole truth. And Zeus, well-pleased, gave the godling a round hat, a golden staff with ribbons, and a pair of winged sandals, so that he could see to the safety of travellers on any road in the world. Later, Zeus's brother Hades made Hermes his herald too, responsible for summoning the dying gently and persuasively into the Underworld—which of course is the final trick the gods play on the living.

Tricksters are common in Africa. Tales of tricksters like Ananse (the Spider), the Rabbit (the ancestor of the American trickster Br'er Rabbit), or the Cock all elicit laughter in African villages, and they are eminently creative, but they also represent a certain perversion of human nature, a tendency toward greediness, brutality, and the ridiculous. It is for this reason that they are often depicted with physical deformities.

This is a Bondei tale of the trickster Cock.

The Cock

Shundi the cockatoo wanted to be friends with the cock, and the cock said that would be nice. In a few days Shundi sent word that he would visit the cock's house with his wives. When they arrived, Shundi was given a goat which they ate every day that Shundi and his wives stayed there. Later, as was custom, the cock sent word to Shundi that he and his wife would visit the next day. And when he arrived, Shundi provided him with a feast of maggots which they all ate during the cock's visit.

Sometime later, Shundi again sent word that he would be visiting. So the cock told his wife to fetch some bananas, peel them, and put them in the pot on the fire. Then he told her to pour water on him, which she did, and he hid behind the pot.

"When Shundi arrives, tell him I am in the pot," the cock said.

Soon Shundi arrived, calling out "Hello," and the cock's wife invited him in. He sat on a stool near the door and asked where the cock was.

"He's in the pot," the cock's wife said, "boiling with the bananas." Before Shundi could say anything, the cock popped up from behind the pot and told Shundi he had been in it, boiling. Shundi was impressed. That night they ate the bananas and Shundi went home.

Soon the cock sent word to Shundi that he was on his way to his house. Shundi told one of his wives to put bananas in the pot and to put him in too.

"But you will die," she said.

Shundi said he wouldn't and into the pot he went. Soon the cock arrived and asked where Shundi was.

"In the pot," was the answer.

"No. What is this you're saying?"

"It is true," the wife said, and they looked in the pot. Shundi was, of course, of yesterday, dead, boiled. His wives all wept and went to the homes of their fathers, and the cock went home as well.

Sometime later, the cock struck up a friendship with a leopard, and they began exchanging visits in the prescribed manner. On one occasion, the leopard arrived and asked where the cock was.

"He is outside, waiting for the shepherds to come back with his head when they bring the goats home." The leopard was surprised and went outside to see. Now, the cock had stuck his head under his wing, so it looked like it had been cut off. When the shepherds arrived with the flock of goats, the cock popped his head out from under his wing and greeted the leopard.

''Where were you?" he asked.

"I sent my head off with the shepherds," the cock said. "Now they have brought it back." The two friends feasted that night on a goat and the leopard went home, thinking how clever his friend was to cut off his head and not die as a result.

So when the cock announced his next visit, the leopard instructed his wife to cut his head off and give it to the shepherds. His wife protested, saying he would die, but the leopard said he wouldn't.

"Tell the cock, when he comes, that I am outside waiting for the shepherds to come back with my head."

So the people came and cut off the leopard's head with an axe and he died on the spot.

Soon the cock arrived. "Anyone home?" he asked. The leopard's wife explained that he was outside waiting for his head. When the shepherds returned, the people found the headless leopard, dead as a rock, and they buried him. While everybody mourned, the cock went home, and nowadays everyone knows not to make friends with the wily cock. That is also why leopards hate fowl. Whenever they find them, they eat them.

A popular African trickster is Ananse the Spider. Ananse is traditionally seen as a mediator between the people and the sky-god Nyame. He even improves on certain aspects of creation. It was he who convinced Nyame to give the people rain to soften the power of the sun and night to provide a time for rest. Like many Native American tricksters, he is a rogue. He even manages to steal away Nyame's daughter, whom he marries. Ananse is usually considered the first king. Like Osiris, Jesus, and other culture heroes, he is also in some sense divine. In this Ashanti myth, Ananse, with the help of his wife, obtains the story-telling ability—the mastery of the mysteries of language—that is a part of the trickster-shaman's power.

Ananse (I)

Ananse the Spider took it into his head that he would like to
know the stories known only to Nyankonpon, the sky-god. So
he went to the sky-god's dwelling and offered to buy the
stories.

"You?" the sky-god said. "A tribeless person like you?
What makes you think you can buy them when many great
villages haven't been able to raise the purchase price?"

Ananse asked what, exactly, the price was, and the sky-
god said the price was the Python, the Leopard, the Fairy, and
the Hornets. And Ananse said that was fine; he would bring all
those and throw in his old mother for good measure. He went
home and plotted with his wife Aso who told him how to catch
the Python.

Armed with a branch from a palm tree and a string of
creeper, Ananse went down to the stream and found Python,
telling him that he and Aso had argued about just how long
Python was.

"Bring that stick over here and measure me," Python said
and he uncoiled himself, lying flat on the ground. Ananse put
the branch beside Python and then, in a trice, wound the
creeper around Python and the stick, tying him from tail to
head, and carried him off to the sky-god.

Later, at Aso's suggestion, he went off with a gourd filled
with water, looking for the Hornets. Finding a swarm, he
sprinkled water on them. Then he poured the rest of the water
on himself and covered his head with a plaintain leaf.

"Look," Ananse said, "the rains have come. I am safe
under this leaf, but shouldn't you fly into this gourd so the rain
won't batter you?" Gratefully, the hornets did so and Ananse
slapped the leaf over the gourd's mouth and took the Hornets
to the sky-god.

Next, Ananse dug a hole in the ground along the trail
frequented by Leopard, and covered it with sticks. The next
day he returned to the hole and found that Leopard had fallen
in. Ananse was delighted, cavorting on the edge, accusing

Leopard of falling in because he was drunk. "I could help you get out, but if I did," Ananse said, "you would eat my children."

"No, no," Leopard said. "I promise I wouldn't do such a thing."

So Ananse cut two sticks and put them in the pit, like steps. Leopard began to climb up and as his head rose above the edge of the pit, Ananse slashed him with his knife. Leopard fell to the bottom of the pit, and Ananse hauled him off to the sky-god.

Back at home, Ananse carved a small doll called an Akua and covered it with sticky resin from a tree. Then he pounded yams into mash and put it into the doll's hand and, tying a string to it, took it to the base of the odum tree where the fairies are known to play. Soon enough, some fairies came and one of them asked the doll if she could eat some of the mash. Ananse tugged the string, making the doll's head nod.

The fairy ate some of the mash and thanked the doll, which remained silent. "I thanked her," the fairy said to her sisters, "but she doesn't answer. How rude!"

"Slap her face," her sisters said, and the fairy did so, finding that her hand was stuck to the doll's head.

"Slap her again, and she'll let go," her sisters said, and again she did so. Again her hand stuck.

"Push it with your stomach," the sisters advised, and the fairy pushed and, of course, got stuck again. So Ananse grabbed the fairy, tied her up and went home. There, he told his mother that he was taking her to the sky-god. Carrying both the old woman and the fairy, Ananse went to the sky-god and demanded the stories be given to him.

The sky-god called a council of elders and explained that Ananse the Spider had paid the price—Python, the Hornets, Leopard, and a Fairy. Also, as promised, he had brought his old mother. The elders sang Ananse's praises and the sky-god handed over the stories.

"From now on," he said, "they will not be called the sky-god's stories. They will be known as Spider stories."

In this Krachi tale of Ananse, the trickster is a metaphor for human cleverness and human limitations in the face of sky-god power. The trickster, dressed in the shamanic costume of a bird and possessed of a magic bag, brings out the sun and also the blight of blindness.

Ananse (II)

Once long ago, when Ananse and the other animal people seved as members of the court of Wulbari, who was god and heaven, the Spider boasted that he had more sense than god himself. Wulbari overheard this and decided to teach the braggart a lesson. He summoned Ananse to him and said, "You must go and bring me *something.*"

Ananse was puzzled. What, he wondered, was *something?* He asked Wulbari to elaborate but Wulbari only laughed. "If you have more sense than I do, you should know that."

So Ananse went down to earth to find *something* and called together all the birds. From each one he took a feather, fashioning a fine multicolored robe. Thus adorned, he went back to heaven and climbed a tree next to Wulbari's house. When Wulbari came out, he saw the wondrous multicolored bird in his tree and called all the animal people, asking them if they knew the name of this bird that was as bright as the rainbow. No one knew, and one of the animal people suggested that Ananse might know. But Wulbari said he had sent Ananse off on a mission—to find *something.*

Well, of course, everyone wanted to know what *something* was, and Wulbari said, "What I had in mind was the sun, the moon, and darkness."

Everyone laughed at how clever Wulbari was and how hopeless Ananse's task was. The braggart was surely getting his comeuppance. But on the contrary, Ananse, sitting in the tree in his bright feathers, had heard what *something* was, so he went away on his mission.

No one knows exactly where he went, or how he managed, but before long he had the sun, the moon, and darkness in his sack which he carried triumphantly back to Wulbari's house.

"Did you find *something*, Ananse?"

"Yes indeed," Ananse said, and pulled out the darkness. Everything went black. No one, not even Wulbari, could see a thing. Next, Ananse pulled the moon out of his sack and everyone could now see a little bit. Next Ananse pulled out the sun. It was so bright that those who looked at it went blind. Those who had looked in another direction went blind in one eye. Only those who had happened to blink kept their eyesight.

And that is how blindness came into the world, along with the sun, the moon, and the night—*something* that Wulbari wanted and Ananse had enough sense to bring for him.

A trickster of the African Yoruba people is Esu-Elegbara or sometimes Legba, and, as Henry Louis Gates, Jr., has pointed out, there are New World versions of him, brought during the years of the slave trade, in Brazil, Cuba, Haiti, and elsewhere. This trickster is the container of the "word," the mysteries of verbal and nonverbal communication as well as of fertility. Like the shaman-trickster of the ancient Les Trois Frères cave, he is a dancer—as Gates has called him, "a mask-in-motion," who conveys his essence "by his phallic dance of regeneration, of creation, of translation" (20). Legba-Esu, like Hermes, is literally a penetrator of the dark world of the unknown. And, like Hermes, he is the guardian of crossroads. Among the Fon people of Dahomey, his penetrating herm-like phallic symbol stands outside all tribal dwellings.

This is a Fon story of Legba.

Legba (Esu-Elegbara)

In a much earlier time, God lived here on earth, and he had a son, Legba, with him to do his bidding. Every now and then, God told Legba to do something that was harmful, and of course the people blamed Legba and came to hate him. On the other hand, when something good happened, they never gave Legba credit; instead, they praised God for his benevolence and generosity.

Legba began to grumble to himself about this and one day he confronted God.

"I have been obedient," Legba said. "All this time I have been obedient and carried out your wishes. And it only gets me trouble. I don't think it's fair. I get blamed and I am just carrying out the divine will."

God smiled and replied that the ruler of a kingdom should be thanked for all the good things that happen, and his servants blamed for evil. "That," he said, "is how it always has been and always will be."

Legba said nothing, merely bowed, his thoughts turning to sedition. Now God had a garden of legendarily fine yams, of which he was very proud indeed, and Legba explained that, in his recent patrols, he had heard that thieves were planning to plunder it. So God called everyone together before him and glowered out at them, saying, "Anyone who steals my yams will be killed. Is that understood?" And he sent everyone away.

That night, Legba stole into God's house while he slept and took his sandals. He put them on and went out into God's garden where, quickly, he took all the yams. Thanks to a rain earlier that evening, the footprints he left behind were clear and crisp in the wet earth.

The next morning, Legba came running to God's house, shouting that some malefactor had stolen the yams. "But," he said ingratiatingly, "it should be very easy to find the thief because he left footprints behind him." God summoned everybody but no one's feet fit the prints, which were far too big.

"This may seem strange," Legba said, "but is it possible, sir, that you yourself took the yams, walking in your sleep?"

"You rascal!" God barked, "of course I didn't." But Legba simply shrugged and looked pointedly at God's feet. The people all looked at God's feet as well so, exasperated, he agreed to put his foot in one of the tracks and dispel all this nonsense. When the people all saw that it was a perfect match, they began to exclaim how God had stolen from himself.

God retorted that his son had tricked him and, in high dudgeon, left the earth, telling Legba to come to the sky every night and give him an account of what had happened that day in the world below.

Often the African trickster is less of a shamanic or god figure than a troublemaker. One gets the sense in some of the African tales, as in some of the Native American ones, that the trickster is a figure who once played a significant role—back at the time of the creation—but who in more orderly village-oriented societies has outlasted his welcome. This is certainly true of the well-known Kaffir cycle of Hlakanyana.

Hlakanyana

One day, the wife of the village chief, who was childless at the time, heard what seemed to be a ringing in her ears. She listened more closely and it seemed to be a voice. Over and over, it said, "Bear me, mother, before the meat of my father is all eaten."

The woman was amazed, for unborn children do not speak, so she cleaned out her ears with a stick. But the voice kept calling out. Soon she gave birth to a tiny little boy with the face of an old man, and this strange little person immediately went to his father's corral, saying, "Father, give me some meat."

The chief did not think he had a son and told the little person to go away. But Hlakanyana (for that was his name) persisted in demanding meat. Finally the chief got angry at these importunings and trampled him into the earth, leaving him for dead. But Hlakanyana rose up, still asking for meat, and the chief threw him some in hopes that he would go away. Instead, Hlakanyana offered to carry all the men's meat back to their huts, and thus began his life of trickery.

For he took all the meat to his mother's house and smeared blood on the eating mats in the huts of the men. Seeing this, the men asked Hlakanyana what had happened to their meat and he replied that it must have been eaten by dogs. The men were angry that their wives and children had not kept a better watch, so they thrashed them all. And later that night, Hlakanyana ate all the meat, telling his mother that it had been eaten by dogs.

Soon Hlakanyana thought up another trick. He came upon an old man near a stream and persuaded him to fetch some water for him. While the old man was at the stream's edge, Hlakanyana ate the meat from the old man's pot and filled it with dung. When the old man returned, he said he was tired and fell asleep. Hlakanyana smeared fat on his old lips and put a bone next to him. At that point, the village men arrived and Hlakanyana said it was time to eat. When the men looked in the pot they were disgusted to find only dung.

"What happened to the meat?" they demanded, and Hlakanyana pointed to the old man, sleeping, his lips greasy with fat. So the men killed him. But some children had been watching and explained that it was Hlakanyana who had taken the meat, so Hlakanyana fled, beginning a long journey of deception and lies by which he fooled people, stealing their meat and getting them in trouble.

On one occasion, he challenged a boy to see who could stay under water longest. Both dived in the river, but Hlakanyana came up immediately and ate all the boy's birds, leaving only the heads.

Another time, Hlakanyana met an old woman and told her

he could make her young. Elated, the old woman did his bidding, fetching some water for her pot. Hlakanyana built a fire under the pot and said, "First, you must put me in the pot and cook me for a little while. Then you must get in and cook for a little while."

The old woman, hoping to regain her youth, agreed and put Hlakanyana in the pot where he sat until the water got hot. "Take me out," he said. "I've cooked long enough." The old grandmother took him out and got in herself, soon asking to be taken out.

"Not yet, grandmother. It isn't time yet."

So the old woman died in the pot. Hlakanyana threw away her bones and put on her clothes, and before long her two sons returned from the hunt.

"Whose meat is this in the pot?" they asked, and Hlakanyana told them it was theirs. They began to eat, and one said, "This looks like our mother's toe." The other said, "And this looks like her finger."

Hlakanyana realized that he would soon be found out, so he tiptoed out of the hut. A little way off, he paused and shouted, "You fools! You're eating your own mother! Who ever heard of such a thing?" And he fled. The two sons chased him with their spears and dogs and just as they were about to seize him, he turned himself into a rock alongside a stream. One of the sons picked up the stone and said that if he could find Hlakanyana, he would throw the stone at him. With that, he threw the stone into the river where it turned back into Hlakanyana, who laughed and continued his journey.

All journeys must eventually come to an end, and Hlakanyana's ended this way.

He had returned to his home village and went out to tend his father's calves, plotting to kill some and eat his fill. On the way, he met a large turtle and asked it where it was going.

"To that large stone over there," the turtle said.

"That could tire you out," Hlakanyana said. "Let me carry you." Happily the turtle climbed on his back and Hlakanyana took him to his mother's hut, with the idea of dropping him in the boiling pot. He asked his mother to take the turtle off his back, but it held on tight. She struggled but it clung

fast. So she heated up some fat and poured it on the turtle
which let go immediately, and the fat sluiced over Hlakanyana, burning him to death.

Another highly reprehensible trickster, who nevertheless is
the creative "father" of the people, is the Bantu giant-
transformer Dikithi.

Dikithi

He was known as the Great Dikithi, and all the animals and
people were in awe of him, but he was an accomplished thief.
He had but one eye, one arm, and one leg, but this did nothing to diminish his skills and often he feasted on the cattle of
others.

One day he dug a hole in the path frequented by the
elephants, covered it with brush and threw his pants into a
nearby tree. When the elephants came along, he sang to them,
begging them to get his pants out of the tree for him. As they
neared the tree, the elephants fell into the pit, and Dikithi
killed them with his spear. He told his children to carry the
elephant meat home which they did, and set about making a
great feast. Others from the village came by and Dikithi refused to let them have any meat. He decided to take his family
and leave the village.

His wife said she wished to have her mother come with
them, but Dikithi forbade it, and they left. But the old woman
followed them, haunting their night-time camps. Finally,
Dikithi grew angry, killed the old woman and covered her
with a pot. After they had gone further on their journey, Hare
(who had accompanied them) saw that a pot was missing, so he
went back to find it. With the pot removed, the old woman

revived and continued her pursuit, singing, "You have taken my daughter. I will follow you."

Dikithi heard her and set the grass on fire to keep her away. She thrashed at the fire with her skirt, shrieking at Dikithi, "I'll get you. I'll cut off your balls."

Seeing that the old woman was still in pursuit, Dikithi and his wife climbed a tree. The old woman came near and began chopping down the tree, repeating her threat. Dikithi called upon the locusts to swarm over his mother-in-law and bite her, which they did, but the old woman thrashed them with her skirt and drove them away.

Dikithi called for the Lion to come but the old woman drove him off as well, still shouting, "I'll cut off your balls, Dikithi."

So Dikithi, with the help of some birds, built a fire around her and burned her to death, making a whistle from her leg-bone. Then, as Dikithi played the whistle, his father appeared and asked to be given the whistle.

"Only," Dikithi said, "if you come up the tree." He lowered a rope and told his father to put it around his neck. The old man did so and Dikithi began to haul him up the tree.

"It hurts my neck," the old man cried, but Dikithi persisted. And when the old man was near the top of the tree, Dikithi took out his knife and cut the rope. The old man, Dikithi's father, fell to his death.

Climbing down from the tree, Dikithi said to his wife, "That old man's stomach is full of meat." He called on the Vulture to open up the stomach, but it was too hard. He called on the Heron but it broke his beak. Even the Eagle could not open up the old man's stomach. So Dikithi sent a small red bird down to the corpse. It entered the old man's mouth and went through him, coming out the anus, and the old man's stomach opened up.

Dikithi called all the animals and people together and they feasted, and the Great Dikithi told them that they could all stay there and live in his village.

The most popular tricksters among American Indians are Coyote, Raven, and a creature often perceived as a spider, called
Iktome (or Iktomi) among the Sioux. In much of the world,
including parts of North America, the raven is considered an
ill-omen, possibly associated with the fact that ravens are major agricultural pests, but in the far North and the Pacific
Northwest (where agriculture is limited to nonexistent), the
raven is something of a culture hero, a creator as well as a
troublemaker. Among the Eskimo, Raven played a major cos-
mogenic role. Among the Athabascans and the tribes of the
Pacific Northwest, his role as the oversexed and ever-hungry
trickster is more prominent. This latter role may be associated
with the raven's evident playfulness: the bird is known for
what seem joyful aerial acrobatics, and it is often seen taunting
wolves as in a child's game. The spider, of course, in its very
weirdness, speaks for itself. And the coyote, often seen alone,
and often seen to vanish, has always been quintessentially a
survivor. (Rather then submit to the eradication programs of
western ranchers, the coyote instead has spread as far east as
Maine and now inhabits every state but Hawaii.) Whatever
their appeal, however, these creatures came to bespeak an
important element in the American Indian view of human
nature and society.

Raven (I)

One day the son of an old couple came running in the house
and excitedly announced that a stranger had arrived at the
landing. He wore many bone beads on his garments and so he
must be very important. Perhaps he would make a good
brother-in-law.

The old couple were delighted, since they had long been

hoping a wealthy man would come along and marry their only daughter. So the mother raced down to the landing and spread wood chips along the muddy shore to make the stranger's way easier for him. Soon she had invited him in to share a feast and sat him next to the daughter.

The stranger pointed to the dog which the family kept tied up in a corner of their home and sniffed, "I can't possibly eat anything while that animal is in here." Such a haughtly complaint could come only from someone of the highest rank and the most fastidious upbringing, so the mother took the dog out of the camp and killed it. The feast then went forward, and the old couple were pleased to see that the wealthy stranger indeed seemed smitten by their daughter and spent the night with them.

The following morning, the mother went out to collect wood and noticed that the body of the dog was surrounded with bird tracks in the earth, and its eyeballs had been plucked out. Suspicion struck: Raven, the Deceiver, often appeared in human form. Perhaps this was one of his outrageous deceptions.

She returned to her house and demanded that everyone take off their mocassins and show their feet. As he slipped off his moccasins, the stranger created a minor distraction and slipped them back on so quickly that no one noticed his scaly, four-toed feet.

To avoid any further prying, the stranger who indeed was Raven, demanded that the daughter leave with him right away on a bridal trip of a few days, after which they would return. Right after they set out in his canoe with Raven seated in the bow, it began to rain, and the bride noticed that her new husband's back was turning from white to black, as if something were being washed off. Fearing she had been duped, she tied the tail of his coat to a crossbar and asked to be set ashore for a moment to relieve herself.

Of course, once she was ashore she took off through the trees, headed for home. After plenty of time had passed for any woman to pee, Raven himself grew suspicious and decided to follow her. But he found that his coat was tied to the canoe, so he had to resume his true bird form. He flew out over the forest and, spotting the girl, swooped down over her head, cawing gaily: "Ha! I cheated you!" And with that, he flew away.

The Brulé Sioux tell many stories about Iktome, the spider-like trickster, from whose mind sex was rarely absent.

Iktome

Iktome's eye had been caught by an especially beautiful young woman whose ignorance of the ways of men and women was reputed to be as intact as her virginity. He longed to sample this fresh fruit, and so he dressed himself in the clothes of a woman and sought her out, finding her on the edge of a stream, preparing to cross it.

"Let's wade across together, my young friend," Iktome said in the quavering voice of an old woman.

The girl smiled and they lifted up their robes and stepped into the water.

"Your legs," the girl said. "They're very hairy."

Iktome sighed. "Yes, it happens with age."

As the water grew deeper, they hiked up their robes a bit farther, and the girl tittered. "Your backside is hairy too," she said.

"Yes, it happens to some of us older people."

The water grew still deeper, and when Iktome hiked his robe up yet farther, the girl gasped.

"What's that? That thing hanging between your legs."

Iktome stopped in the water. "It's a growth, like a wart. It was put there by a sorcerer." He sighed. "It's heavy, and it gets in the way, I can assure you, my young friend. And it hurts, I wish I could get rid of it."

"We could cut it off," the girl suggested.

"Oh, no, NO," Iktome said, cringing slightly. "The sorcerer . . . well, there's only one way to get rid of it. If we put it there, between your legs. . . ."

The girl thought this a strange, even unattractive idea, but she decided that women should help one another and agreed. So they crossed to the other bank and lay down on the soft grass. Soon enough, Iktome rolled over on top of the girl and entered her.

"Ooh," she said. "That hurts."

"It hurts me even more," panted Iktome and soon he was finished and rolled off.

"Look," the girl said, smiling. "It's working. It's gotten smaller."

"We'll do it again, and maybe it will disappear altogether," Iktome said, and again he mounted the girl.

"It's grown again," she said. "But it doesn't hurt me so much. Does it hurt you still?"

Iktome labored away, and when he finished he said, "Yes, little sister, the pain is very great, but I am brave. I can take it."

Twice more Iktome labored and afterward, the girl said: "I don't know, older sister. It is still there. We don't seem to be making much progress. You may never get rid of that thing."

"Perhaps, but we should keep trying. Do you agree?"

And the girl, who had forgotten now why she had set out across the river, agreed.

Both the Hopi and their neighbors, the Navajo, explain how Coyote played a role in the configuration of the stars above. In each case, the people had emerged into a new, but dark world. For the Hopi, it fell to the Hero Twins to place the stars in heaven; for the Navajo, it was First Man.

The task was arduous, one calling for a great deal of thought and care. And when the first few stars had been placed in careful patterns, such as the Pleiades, Orion, the Milky Way, and a few other notable constellations, Coyote step-danced into the act. Thinking it silly to spend so much time and thought on such a task, he simply picked up the remaining stars and threw them into the sky, scattering them there without reason or order.

Beyond his sometimes blundering, sometimes helpful cosmic role, Coyote more often than not deals in more mundane matters, tricking or attempting to trick other creatures including men and women. Often his tricks backfire, and he may find himself dismembered or (not unlike the cartoon character who wars ceaselessly with the Roadrunner) flattened. Yet he never fails to reconstitute himself and continue his anarchic and scatological pranks.

But for the Maida, a band of California Indians, Coyote played a role of fearful darkness.

Coyote

In the beginning, when there was only night and water, a raft brought two persons—Turtle and Earth-Initiate. Working together, they created first some dry land, then the sun and the moon, and the stars, as well as a large tree with many kinds of acorns. Before long, Coyote and his pet, Rattlesnake, emerged of their own accord, and Coyote watched with great interest as Earth-Initiate fashioned all the animals from clay. He watched with even greater interest when Earth-Initiate created the First Man and the First Woman.

Coyote thought it looked pretty easy, so he tried to make some people himself, but they didn't work out because he laughed while he was making them. Earth-Initiate said, "I told you not to laugh," and Coyote told the world's first lie, saying that he hadn't laughed.

Earth-Initiate wanted life to be easy and full for the people he had caused to exist, so every night he saw to it that their baskets were filled with food for the next day. No one had to work; no one got sick. One day, he told the people to go to a nearby lake, and he explained to the First Man that by the time he got there, he would be old.

Sure enough, when the people got to the lake, the First Man was white-haired and bent. He fell in the lake which shook, and the ground underneath roared, and soon he came to the top, a young man again. Earth-Initiate explained to all the people that, when they got old, all they needed to do was to plunge into the lake and they would be young again.

Then one day, Coyote visited the people and they told him how easy life was, how all they needed to do was eat and sleep.

"I can show you something better than that," Coyote said, and told them that he thought it would be better if people got sick and died. The people had no idea what he meant so he suggested that they begin by having a footrace. He told them how to line up to start the race.

At this moment his pet, Rattlesnake, went out along the race course and hid himself in a hole, with just his head sticking up. And then the race began.

Some of the people were faster than others and began to pull ahead from the pack, and one in particular ran the fastest. This was Coyote's son, and Coyote, watching from the sidelines, cheered him on with pride. But then his son came to a hole and Rattlesnake raised his head and bit him on the ankle. The boy, Coyote's son, fell over and within moments was dead.

The people all thought the boy was too ashamed to get up, but Coyote explained that he was dead. Coyote wept—the first tears—and gathered up his son and put him in the lake where the body floated for four days without reviving. So Coyote dug a grave and buried his son and told the people that this was what they would have to do from then on.

Versions of both the shamanic and trickster stages of God remain with us to this day, in several of the cultures whose myths have been discussed here, and they remain in remnant form in the successive stages of God that are treated in the next sections.

II

The Rise of
the Archetype:
Divine Child/
Goddess Consort/
Dying God

The bull-god sacrificed by a priest in ancient Crete, Minoan god seal
(second millennium B.C.E.). (After photograph by Sir Arthur Evans)

The emergence of the Neolithic age out of the Paleolithic occurred gradually in various parts of the world in the transitional period from about 10,000 to 7000 B.C.E. The relatively recent archeological discoveries made at places like Çatal Hüyük and Hacilar and Jericho in the Middle East suggest that the Neolithic lifestyle was firmly established there as early as 7500 B.C.E. The same can be said of the Indus Valley in India.

The Neolithic is a village culture that develops around the new practices of agriculture and the domestication and herding of animals that in many areas first supplemented and then in great part replaced the hunting and gathering that provided for the survival of the earlier Paleolithic people. With agriculture and animal husbandry comes the need for settlement, and with settlement typically come strictly organized burial practices, a communal architectural style, the development of domestic arts like weaving and pottery, further specialization of the work force, including the duties of males and females, a more sophisticated body of myths and rituals, a priestly class to preserve and interpret them, and more particular characterizations of deities to fit the needs, concerns, and conditions of the particular settlements in question.

In the modern age we have direct experience of the differences between the lifestyles of hunter-gatherers and those of the domesticating growers. The Indians of the Great Plains and certain nomadic tribes of Africa and the Middle East, for example, until recently were hunter-gatherers whose mythology was dominated by the hunt and who moved from place to place setting up camps that we associate with tepees and other forms of portable tent architecture. Their religions were dominated by shamans and magic, rather than by priests and dogma. In contrast, the cultures encountered in the American Southwest by Athabascans and other hunter-

gatherers, who arrived in the middle of the second millennium
C.E., were established proto-Neolithic societies whose people
lived in pueblo-like settlements that had much more in common with the communal structures of the Aztecs and Mayans
of the South or with modern-day apartment buildings than
with tepees and tents or hogans. The living arrangement of
the Anasazi of Mesa Verde and Chaco Canyon and their modern Hopi and Rio Grande Pueblo descendants in several ways
resembles what archeology suggests might have existed at
Çatal Hüyük and Hacilar. These cultures are typically ma-
trilineal, they all have prominent Goddess figures in their
mythologies, and they are all agriculturally based and committed to domestic crafts and the raising of domestic animals.
They all have strict burial practices and live in adobe-based
houses built in blocks one upon the other, with particular
spaces—often underground—designated for religious purposes (kivas). In addition, they are all dominated by priesthoods that preserve and direct a complex system of rituals
associated with the seasons and a highly developed mythological system. The shamans and tricksters of the past are assimilated into the priestly rituals and, in the case of the American
Indians in question, into dancing animal spirits and sometimes
phallic clown figures.

As to the mythology itself, where the Paleolithic period
was probably dominated by an animistic rather than a specifically personified Earth Goddess, the early Neolithic settlements seem to have recognized a more clearly individualized
Mother Goddess, who eventually took the familiar forms of
figures such as Inanna, Cybele, and Hathor, and who, though
clearly related to the old Earth Goddess, had specific biogra-
phies attached to them, where their originator probably did
not.

As for God, the early and ubiquitous animal master–
victim/shaman/trickster grows in the Neolithic age into many
masks of an archetype of the Dying God who will share the
mythological stage with his Mother Goddess consort until the
rise of the great patriarchal sky-gods who take mythological
power later. Even long after the establishment of the par-
triarchal pantheons of Babylon, Egypt, India, and elsewhere,

Goddess and her son-lover remained a pervasive force in the religions and lives of peoples who practiced the arts of agriculture and animal domestication. As was the case with the Paleolithic age, we have no myths from the preliterate peoples of the early Neolithic age. We have to wait until writing develops in Sumer and Egypt in the fourth millennium for the actual myths. But we can imagine what the mythology of the period would have been like by examining the archeological evidence, by considering the myths of Goddess and her consort that were recorded in the first millennia of literacy, and by studying the myths of those later peoples mentioned earlier, whose Neolithic-type religions and domestic practices continued into the modern age.

To understand the development of the Neolithic masks of God from the old shaman-trickster god of the caves, we would do well to consider first the Neolithic descendants of the cave paintings. Where the Paleolithic artist painted and carved in the sacred Goddess womb-caves, the Neolithic ones worked in the sacred Goddess temples such as the ones discovered at Çatal Hüyük and in the underground kivas or man-made ceremonial "caves" of the Anasazi and their descendants—caves that surely take their deepest symbolic significance from the myths of the Spider Woman–type Goddess and the emergences of the people in a distant past from what might well be called the "womb" of the Great Mother Earth.

Figurines, paintings, and engravings found in places like Çatal Hüyük indicate that Goddess power of the Paleolithic era remained in place in the early Neolithic. The vast majority of artifacts found in these sites are Goddess artifacts. But there is also a significant male presence in several figures that point back to and are, in effect, elaborations of the old shaman God of the caves. The male figure in question is often a bull.

There are many early Neolithic examples of the Goddess–Bull combination—a bull's head with the goddess on figurines and walls is common. In a striking shrine bas-relief at Çatal Hüyük, there is a depiction of Goddess giving birth to what appears to be a bull. The shrine walls are decorated with images of her bull-son.

There is also a fusing of bulls with horned serpents and

Goddess birthing the bull (Çatal Hüyük, ca. 7000 B.C.E.). (After James Mellaart)

fish. Lions, too, are associated with these early depictions of Goddess; she is often flanked by them. These golden beasts are in all likelihood representative of the sun, the necessary companion of Goddess in her function as natural provider. And there are lion-headed eagles. There are also bull men and goat men, and a bearded man who rides a bull or who is a bull-centaur of sorts. Many of the bull men and goat men as well as some apparently purely human males are ithyphallic and young. But there are also what appear to be elderly sedate men who are distinctly not ithyphallic and who rest in a posture suggesting sadness or repose. And there are serpents, as there had been with the Paleolithic goddesses.

Rock painting of a man wearing a bull mask. (Tassili Auanrhet, Africa, ca. 6000 B.C.E.). (After Henri Lhote)

Sculpture of a goat-man (Vinca, Yugoslavia, ca. 5000 B.C.E.).(After
Miodrag Djordjević)

It seems logical to assume that this proliferation of animal
figures and animal–human combinations is indeed related to
the older Paleolithic shaman gods, and it seems equally logical
to assume that the new Goddess–Animal God association
points to the idea of a sacred marriage, itself associated with
the new practices of animal mating and agriculture.

The young ithyphallic figures remind us of the ithyphalli-
cism of the cave figures and perhaps suggest the rising aspect
of the natural cycles as the elderly nonithyphallic figures suggest the falling off—the birth in the spring and the dying in
winter, the rising and setting of the sun. The male is thus
given a significant role in the daily life–death cycle and in the
ritual aspect of planting that involves the seed's fertilizing of
the earth and its dying there to be reborn—literally re-erected
or resurrected in the spring—only to be harvested and planted
again.

The development of the Neolothic myths of God in association with the Great Mother's nourishing of the people is

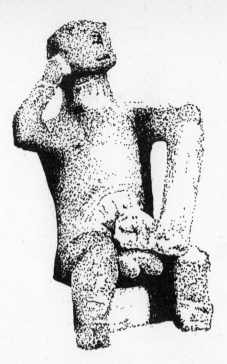

Ithyphallic Young Year God of Renewal holding phallus (Larisa, Greece, ca. 5000 B.C.E.). (After Marija Gimbutas and K. Kónya)

also revealed in the strange rituals and myths of the Dying God that are outlined by Sir James Frazer in his classic work, *The Golden Bough*, in which Frazer discusses the fertility myths of the Middle East and later rituals of a sacrificed king. These myths and rituals cannot help but remind us of the descent into the spirit world of the shaman and the sacrifice of the old animal master. In a society in which there is dependence on the animal for food, the slain animal typically becomes a "willing" victim in a ritual killing, a sacred object, sometimes the generous animal "father." That the consort of a goddess who represents the all-giving earth should be an animal or an animal god, and that he—even sometimes as a king or his scapegoat animal substitute—should be sacrificed to her and replaced by a new and younger god is not surprising. The sacrifice of the god in myth and sometimes of the king or

Old Year God of Decline (Volos, Greece, ca. 5900 B.C.E.). (After Marija Gimbutas and K. Kónya)

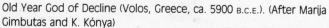

scapegoat in ritual—the ritual-myth of the Year Spirit, the Year God, the Dying God—is the means by which the ritual sacrifice of the hunt now becomes the ritual sacrifice of planting and animal slaughter.

In their creation myth, the Mande people of Mali tell of Faro, who willingly died to atone for his brother's sin of having defiled their mother, Earth. Like so many sacrificed gods, he becomes in his dismembered state the seeds for a renewed nature.

Faro

First God created a single seed, but it failed, so he decided instead to create seed-twins. In this way, the egg of the world

The Neolithic rock shrines of southern Africa contain particularly vivid depictions of the Dying God. In this figure from Zimbabwe, the spirit of the dead god pours forth from his phallus the seeds of new life. (After Frobenius Institute photograph)

was created in two parts which, together, were to procreate. Pleased with this, God made six more seed-twins. Within each of the eight seeds, then, were two essences, one male, the other female. According to God's plan, the eight seeds were to create the four elements and the four cardinal directions, providing the world-to-be with the matter and order from which it could emerge.

But one of the males, who was named Pembra, decided that if he emerged from his seed ahead of all the others, he would be the most important in the creation. So, before gestation had come to an end, Pembra escaped and, having torn off a piece of the placenta that surrounded him, he fell down through space. The piece of placenta with him soon became the earth—but it was a dry place, barren and useless. Seeing he had made a mistake, Pembra returned to heaven and tried to take up his place again in whatever remained of his pla-

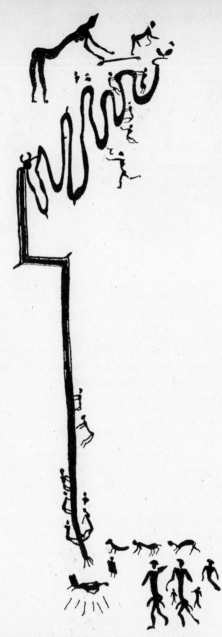

In this second painting from Zimbabwe, the rain–lightning serpent connects the sacrificed "god" on the ground with the goddess above and forms a ladder on which the people and animals can climb to her. (After Frobenius Institute photograph)

centa. But God had changed his remaining placenta into the sun, so Pembra stole some other seeds and returned to the barren earth—his placenta and, in fact, his mother's womb—where he planted them.

Pembra's acts—both theft and incest—turned the earth impure and only one of the stolen seeds grew, in the placenta's blood. All the others died for lack of moisture.

All this while, in heaven, one of the other male twins, named Faro, had been germinating, taking the form of two fishes. One fish bespoke Faro's strength and life, the other his body. To atone for Pembra's sins and to purify the now defiled earth, God sacrificed Faro and sliced his body up into sixty pieces which he cast out into space. The pieces floated down through space and landed on the dry earth where they each soon grew into tall, self-seeding trees.

Seeing this, God brought Faro back to life in heaven, gave him human form, and sent him back to earth in an ark which soon fetched up against the mountain that encircles the world—now what we call the land of the Mande. There, from Faro's placenta, arose the original ancestors of the people. These ancestors, like Faro, had both a life force and a spiritual force within them—each of which had within *them* a male and female form.

But the world was still not perfect. It remained too dry. But then the ancestral smith descended to earth and, seeing the drought, struck a rock with his hammer, asking for rain. Water poured forth from heaven, making the earth pure and fecund, and the water was followed by two fishes, which bespoke Faro. So today, water is the messenger between Faro and mankind, and the people who know this, the Mande and many others, never eat fish from the river or the sea.

Still another god whose somewhat sacrificial death becomes a source of renewal is Wiyot, the consort of the Great Mother of the California Luiseno Indians.

Wiyot

In the beginning there was only Kevish-Atakvish, the space-void. But then things began to fall into forms—time came into being, and the Milky Way. Even so there was no light, just a creative stirring.

But in due course, Kevish-Atakvish made a man, Tukmit, who was the sky, and then the man's sister, Tomaiyovit, who was the earth. Still there was no light, and the brother and sister could not see one another, but they knew each other. They conceived and gave birth to the first elements of creation—valleys, mountains, stones, streams, and everything else that would be needed for worship and ceremonies and cooking.

Then, from earth, came a terrifying meteor. This was Takwish, and with him came his son Towish, the immortal soul of all human beings. And Wiyot came forth and from Wiyot came the people, even though it was still dark.

Earth Mother, Tomaiyovit, made a bright sun to light the world but it was too bright. It terrified the people and had to be hidden away.

The people made more people and they followed the growing earth as it stretched farther and farther outward. Eventually, they came to a place called Temecula and there Tomaiyavit brought out the sun again. The people raised the sun up into the sky above where it followed a regular path each day and wasn't so frightening.

But all was not well. Frog hated Wiyot, the father of the people, because of the strangely shaped legs he had made for her. She spit into Wiyot's water and, after drinking the poison, Wiyot announced that he would die in the spring. During the winter before he died, he told the people all that they needed to know to thrive on earth, and when he did die, a great oak tree grew up from his ashes.

Now Wiyot visits the people each night as the moon and is the center of their celebrations. The people dance for him and cry out, "Wiyot, the father of the people, has risen!"

In the rock and cave paintings of northern Australia there is a
version of the Dying God or at least disappearing god archetype, one associated with the complex system of creative
dreaming that marks the philosophy of the Aborigines.

The Wondjina, the reclining ithyphallic figure, is rain. He
has sunk into the ground and left his image behind as child
seeds who will implant themselves in women. They are the
ancestors. There are many Wondjina. According to the Unum-
bal of northern Kimberley, they were originally discovered by
the Great Cosmic Earth Serpent, Ungud—a form of the
Mother Goddess.

Wondjina

They have been here, you see?

They came into being of their own accord in the beginning, in the Dream Time, and they journeyed over the earth.
But that was after they were found at the bottom of the waters
by the great Ungud.

On their journeys, they brought forth the hills and the
plains, and they brought rain, and when the rocks were still
wet and soft, they lay down on them—not everywhere, you
understand, but here and there in special places, homes—and
left in the rocks impressions of themselves.

They are the Wondjina.

We can see the impressions they left behind in the rocks as
paintings.

Each place, each spring, lake, river, was marked by a
Wondjina who owns that place and lives there still, beneath
the painting, far down in the water in the middle of the earth.
There, in the waters, the Wondjina creates child-germs—each

Wondjina. (After Munich Folk Art Museum photograph)

one a tiny fragment of the Wondjina itself, and therefore of
Ungud too.

Do you see?

And a father comes to such a place and in a dream he finds
a child-germ. In yet another dream, he urges that child-germ
into his wife, and inside her it takes on human form. That
is how lives are made, from these child-germs and from us,
ourselves, and at the end of a life, the germ returns to the
waters where it waits patiently for another turn, another human form.

So, you see, all of us who are descended from a given
Wondjina, one who has left its mark in a place, are the rightful
owners of that place. It is our home. We all go back to the
original Wondjina who lay here in the soft rock in the beginnings of Dream Time. We are part of that impression. We
speak for the Wondjina of whom we are part, saying that I left
my impression here in the rock when I passed through here in
Dream Time.

And so, it is natural that when we come by here, before
the rainy season, we repaint the image in the rock, we refresh
ourself, invigorate ourself. We fill our mouth with water and
spray it on the painting, and it is a gift to us, to the Wondjina,
and to Ungud.

You see how it is?
It is very simple.

∽

At this stage, it is useful to place ourselves mentally in a place like Çatal Hüyük, in the centuries before ca. 7500 B.C.E., and to accelerate the communal thought-process by which we move from the "religion" of the "Sorcerer" of Les Trois Frères and the ubiquitous Earth Goddess to that of the Great Mother and the Dying God.

We can imagine a time when women discovered that it was possible to contain and control in manageable plots what had been wild edible vegetation. These plots had the advantage of a certain predictability and the disadvantage of requiring relatively constant care. With the development of the plow, they required more help in the field from the men. The men plowed the body of the Great Mother so that she could be filled with the seed of last year's dying plants and by some strange mystery the Great Mother gave off new plants, especially if the priests danced and sang for her and perhaps left some of their own body seed or even spilled some blood there. When men or women died, it seemed that the Great Mother expected them to be returned to her, but the priests said she would like younger flesh sometimes. The priests told stories of how this all began.

This is one of those stories as told by the Ojibway Indians.

Mondawmin

When the youth Wunzh reached the proper age, his father built him a lodge in a remote place where he could fast undisturbed and find his guardian in life. It was spring of the year and, in the first days of his fast, Wunzh walked the woods each morning, musing on the first shoots of plants and flowers, coming alive in the warming earth.

He hoped this would store his mind with pleasant thoughts for his dreams each night. Often, on these strolls, he found himself wondering how these plants grew, some of them sweet like berries, others poisonous, yet others full of medicine. Perhaps, if he knew more about such things, he could help his people. Perhaps they might not have to rely on the luck of the hunt or the occasional fish caught from opaque waters.

As the days went by, Wunzh grew too weak for such wanderings and instead lay in his lodge, praying that he would dream of something that would help his people. In his increasing dizziness, he permitted himself the thought that while the Great Spirit had made all things, including the people, he could have made things a bit easier for them.

On the third day of his fast, as he lay in his lodge, he saw a figure descend from the sky—a figure richly dressed in yellow and green garments of many shades, with a great plume of golden feathers waving on its head. With dreamlike grace, it arrived in Wunzh's lodge.

"The Great Spirit sent me to you, my friend," said the figure. "He takes note that your prayers are unusual. You don't seem to want the glory of the warrior, but instead merely something for the good of your people." The visitor went on to explain that this was possible. The condition was that Wunzh wrestle with his visitor.

At first, Wunzh's heart sank. He was already weak from fasting. What hope did he have . . . ? But gathering his courage, he engaged the figure, and they wrestled until Wunzh felt utterly exhausted. Abruptly, the figure stopped, smiled, and said, "That's enough for now. You did well, I will come again to try you." He disappeared, ascending into the light of the sun.

The following day he came again, and once again challenged Wunzh who by now was even weaker. But it seemed that the weaker his body was, the greater his courage and determination. Again they wrestled, long and hard, and again the visitor broke it off, promising to come again for the final trial. Wunzh collapsed in an exhaustion near death.

The next day, after the third and final trial had begun, the heavenly visitor stopped and declared himself beaten. He sat down next to the youth and told him the Great Spirit was pleased with his courage. Now he would receive the instructions he had prayed for.

"Tomorrow," the visitor said, "is your seventh day of fasting. Your father will come with some food for strength and I will come again and you will win. Afterward, you must strip my clothes from me, put me on the ground, and take away all the weeds. Then you must bury me there. Do not let weeds grow there, but come from time to time and see if I have returned. And then you will have your wish and be able to teach your people what you want them to know."

In the morning, Wunzh's father came with food, and the youth said he would wait until sundown to eat it. And when the visitor came again, Wunzh seized him with strength that amazed the youth, threw him down on the ground and stripped away his rich yellow and green clothes. Seeing that the figure was dead, he buried him as he had been told to, and returned to his father's lodge to eat.

In the days that followed, Wunzh would go off unannounced to the spot where he had buried his friend and kept the weeds away. Toward the end of summer, he came to the spot and found that his old lodge had disappeared. In its stead was a tall, graceful plant, with clusters of yellow on its side, long green leaves, and a graceful plume of gold nodding from the top.

"It is my friend," Wunzh said to himself, and suddenly knew his friend's name: Mondawmin. He ran to fetch his father and told him that this was what he had dreamed for in his fast. If the people cared for his friend the way Wunzh had been instructed, they would no longer have to rely only on the hunt or the waters. With that, he showed his father how to tear off the yellow clusters, as he had torn off the garments before, and he showed how to hold the ears to the fire to turn them brown. The whole family then gathered for a feast upon this newly grown presence in their lives, and expressed their lasting thanks to the spirit, the beautiful visitor, who had given it to them.

And so corn came into this world.

Meanwhile, men were discovering that although the hunt was exciting, it was unpredictable; sometimes the people had to go without meat. The men had seen the animals mate, and they knew how they themselves mated. They knew that they entered the female and left seed there and that sometime later, by some miracle, new young men and women appeared. The men thought it might be possible to contain and control some animals to be used as a constant food source. They learned that the bulls would fight each other to become chief bull; they learned that it was sometimes best to slaughter an old bull to make way for a younger and more virile one. But they knew from their hunting days—they still hunted from time to time—and from old stories, like the Bear Man story we heard earlier, that the killed animal must be respected, that as the Great Mother provided, so did the father bull. When it was time for the new bull to be installed as animal master, it was necessary to call on the priests, in their animal costumes, to dance and sing over the dying bull. The dying bull was really a god, the son of the Great Mother, and the Great Mother was in the cow as she was in everything else.

The people in Crete told a strange story about how the Queen was really the Mother and how once she asked the magician Daedalus to make her a costume so that she could be entered by the sacred bull of the god—the god, himself, of course. Daedalus did that, and the Queen gave birth to a violent bull-man son. This son, the Minotaur, was sacrificed later by the hero Theseus in his lair, the Labyrinth.

What almost certainly happened in the transitional period between the Paleolithic and the Neolithic is that the old wild shaman/animal master/trickster evolved through the priestly filter into the more contained and controlled god consort of the also newly controlled and contained Great Mother. These deities, now established in man-made temples, became the protectors and foci of a village-oriented settled life. Their new characteristics and their new married relationship mirrored the new agricultural and animal husbandry practices, and they were incarnated in the Queen and her virile king.

That the god of these ancient people is a serpent or a bull or a lion or a goat is appropriate, since each of these animals is associated traditionally with fertility. The phallic serpent especially, who is of the dark earth and who sloughs off its skin each year and is born again, is an appropriate symbol. He is the shaman-trickster par excellence, an obvious candidate to become the Goddess' spouse, as he is already privy to the dark confines of the earth-womb. But the bull is as apt a candidate. He is sheer power, masterful virility. In India he would become the bull-god Siva, the great dancer of life, at once destroyer and greatest of yogis—transformer, spiritual trickster—and husband of Parvati, the Daughter of the Mountain. The symbol of Siva and Parvati is the joined lingam and yoni, the phallus and vulva of the sacred pair. Egyptian pharaohs were called "Bull of His Mother," and the Mother was the Cow Goddess Hathor (the House of Horus). In the tomb—itself the symbol of the womb of the Mother—the dead king became Osiris and conceived the new god, the son-lover Horus, the new pharaoh. In Greece, Poseidon the bull-god lived in the maternal sea; his followers and victims were bull dancers in Crete who would confront the great labyrinthian monster Minotaur within the earth. As for the goat, he too is a dancer and a singer, a reminder of that horned phallic shaman-dancer of the Trois Frères cave. In Greece, he would give his name to the ritual sacrifice of the divine king which was tragedy ("goat song") and was accompanied by the stately song-dance of the choral dithyramb. Remember, too, that the most famous of the tragic heroes, Oedipus, was the son-lover of the sacred queen of Thebes to whom he was married after the death of the king who was his father.

That the Goddess is the Mother of the animal-god victims who become her spouse is obvious, since she is the Mother of, the container of, all things. As the embodiment of fertility, Goddess must be "plowed" and "seeded," and the survival of the people depends upon the virility of the seed. It is also true that the seed must be sacrificed—planted—buried—before it can give forth fruit as the new son of the Mother. And not surprisingly, the Mother craves a new son-lover each year. She gives life and she takes away life; she is life and death, the total process. Her son-lover who dies in the Neolithic myths is the ancestor of the hero who will descend to the underworld to bring back the boon of new life. The wildness, the magic, the promiscuity of God in his mask as old shaman-trickster have been transformed by the Dying God of the Neolithic period into the controlled and relatively orderly practices of domesticated procreation, agriculture, and animal husbandry. As the wild berries and grasses, the wild animals, and the Great Mother herself have been contained in the village walls, so has God.

Our most ancient source for Neolithic myths is the society that developed at Sumer. The Sumerians were the culturally dominant civilization of the Mesopotamian Fertile Crescent during the fourth and third millennia B.C.E. They were not Indo-European and they were not Semitic. They were among the first if not the first of the literate peoples, inventing and perfecting the cuneiform system of writing that was eventually adapted by most other Near Eastern societies and giving birth to the world's first great body of literature. Our knowledge of this literature—at least in its earliest form—is somewhat limited. Tablets containing the stories of Gilgamesh, the myths, hymns, and songs that are the ancestors of such familiar Judeo-Christian writings as Noah's Flood and the Song of Songs are still being excavated. Most can be dated back only as far as about 2000 B.C.E. Much of our information about the Sumerians and their mythology comes from the works of later cultures clearly influenced by them—particularly the Babylonian and Assyrian-Akkadian cultures—and of Mesopotamia. The sophisticated mythology and literature of the Sumerians was the first High Neolithic literary and religious result of the developing arts and concepts that would seem to have taken form in societies such as the one at Çatal Hüyük.

One of the most important figures in the Sumerian pan-

An ancient Cretan seal shows Goddess, full-breasted, standing on the world mountain, flanked by lions, and being adored by an aroused youth, in all likelihood the new son-lover, the new king who comes to her and will one day be the death-seed of life. (After G. Rachel Levy)

theon, one who lost some of her power as the patriarchal city-state emerged in Mesopotamia, but who nevertheless was always a significant force, was the Great Goddess as Inanna (the Babylonian Ishtar). The male deity particularly associated with Inanna is the Dying God as Dumuzi (the Babylonian Tammuz), the shepherd king.

Dumuzi is the first literary descendant of the sacred death-seed and animal master/Dying God of the world of Çatal Hüyük. He was at once the cluster of dates on the tree of life and the lord of the sheepfold, the shepherd who kept the flock of the Great Goddess, who was herself the tree and the sheepfold that became, in the organized priestly religion, the temple-ziggurat, the world mountain of the Eternal Mother. In this connection we remember the Mountain Mother of Crete and the Mountain Mother as Cybele in Phrygia.

There was, as we shall see, a myth of a somewhat person-

alized Dumuzi, but the Dumuzi we hear of in the hymns of
Sumer was a generic figure, the Bull of Heaven whose reign is
limited by the human condition, by death itself. In each of his
incarnations he is the "sacred son"—for that is what Dumuzi
means—as later each Christian bishop with his symbolic shepherd's crook (crozier) would be the living "son" of the Mother
church, representing the Dying God-shepherd himself. The
bishop exists only to be succeeded upon his departure by
another version of the "lord."

In Sumer, Dumuzi, as the fruit of the Mother's tree, was
also the seed to be planted in the Mother; as her fertilizing
bull, he was the victim to be buried in death within her. He
was the seed who would be resurrected as the fruit, the sacrificed bull who would be resurrected as the newborn animals of
the fold. So it was that he and later versions of him were
represented also by animals other than the bull—the ram, the
goat, and sometimes the lamb or the fish.

The son-lover aspect of Dumuzi is both strange and logical. All beings are children of the Earth—of the eternal
mother. We learn from the ancient hymns that "in his childhood" "in (her) bosom," "the Mother compassionate," "his
wife Inanna gave him rest." This same child Dumuzi, as a
man, becomes the object of the Mother's desires: "Who will
plow my vulva . . . who will plow my wet field?" she cries
out in one hymn. And each spring, upon the god's return from
what the myth will reveal as an annual death-journey, a sacred
marriage of the risen son and his compassionate mother was
celebrated in the Goddess temple. The god had been planted
in his mother's bosom earlier, either as a literally sacrificed
king or as a sacrificed animal. Now the king as Dumuzi or the
priest of Dumuzi if the king and the head priest were not one
and the same, were joined, and Inanna "embraces her beloved
husband."

The ceremonial hymns that tell of the nature of the sacred
joining have echoes in the Song of Songs (Song of Solomon) of
the Hebrew Bible, a series of Sumerian-Babylonian-Egyptian
erotic marriage songs that the Christian church, in an attempt
to assimilate them theologically, saw as an allegory of the
"marriage" between Jesus and his beloved, the church. Be

that as it may, we also find the universal celebration of the union of seed and earth.

"I am the rose of Sharon, and the lily of the valleys," sings the beloved of the Song. "As the apple tree among the trees of the wood, so is my beloved among the sons. I sat down under his shadow with great delight, and his fruit was sweet to my taste." And the lover sings back, "Thou hast ravished my heart, my sister, my spouse; thou hast ravished my heart . . . Thy lips, O my spouse, drop as the honeycomb: honey and milk are under thy tongue; and the smell of thy garments is like the smell of Lebanon." And his love answers, "Awake, O north wind; and come, thou south; blow upon my garden, that the spices thereof may flow out. Let my beloved come into his garden, and eat his pleasant fruits." The wife, whose "navel is like a round goblet, which wanteth not liquor" and whose "belly is like an heap of wheat set about with lilies," tells how she "opened to my beloved; but my beloved had withdrawn himself and was gone . . . I charge you, O daughters of Jerusalem, if ye find my beloved, that ye tell him, that I am *sick* of love." The lost beloved, found, is associated with the new life of spring: "Come, my beloved, let us go forth into the field; let us lodge in the villages. Let us get up early to the vineyards; let us see if the vine flourish, whether the tender grape appear, and the pomegranates bud forth: there will I give thee my loves."

In the earlier Sumerian hymns, the lord Dumuzi sings, "My sister, I would go with you to my garden. . . . There I would plant the sweet, honey-covered seed." And Inanna sings, telling how she went with Dumuzi into the garden and how she "knelt as is proper"—perhaps imitating the coital position of the mammals of the sheepfold—waiting for her lover "who rose to me out of the poplar leaves."

In one hymn we are told that "at the king's lap stood the rising cedar," and we hear Dumuzi praising the fecundity of the goddess:

> O Lady, your breast is your field.
>
> . . .
>
> Your broad field pours out grain.

> . . .
>
> Pour it out for me, Inanna.
> I will drink all you offer.

And Inanna is no less pleased with Dumuzi:

> You have captivated me, let me stand tremblingly before you,
> Lion, I would be taken by you to the bedchamber.

And

> My honey-man, my honey-man sweetens me always.
>
> . . .
>
> My eager impetuous caresser of the navel,
> My caresser of the soft thighs,
> He is the one my womb loves best.

And

> He shaped my loins with his fair hands,
> The shepherd Dumuzi filled my lap with cream and milk,
> He stroked my pubic hair,
> He watered my womb.
> He laid his hands on my holy vulva,
> He smoothed my black boat with cream,
> He quickened my narrow boat with milk
>
> . . .
>
> Now I will caress my high priest on the bed,
> I will caress the faithful shepherd Dumuzi,
> I will caress his loins, the shepherdship of the land,
> I will decree a sweet fate for him.

That "sweet fate" is to be the constantly renewed insemi-
nator of her fields. It is a fate that involves the mystery of the
planted seed, the mystery of death. This descendant of the
phallic shaman–animal master must, like his ancestor, make
the journey to the other world.

Dumuzi

And so, having faced death in the underworld, having died in the underworld, having suffered the manifold indignities of death, having mourned all that she had had to leave behind— her power, her finery, her breath and, perhaps most grievous, the precious caresses of her glorious son and virile consort, young Dumuzi—having given up all such hope in the underworld, Inanna ascended into the blessed light of this world. With her were the pale demons who turned life into death, a bloodless, voracious band sent along to aid in her search for that substitute life she had promised to the lipless queen of the underworld.

No sooner had Inanna passed through the gates from the Land of No Return, clad again in her silken robes and shimmering jewels, than an old man approached with tears of elation coursing down the seams of his face. So pleased was he to see the Goddess returned, and with her the pale green buds on the branches, the brightening of the sky, that he fell on his knees and reached out to her. But the demons began gibbering, eager fires burning in their eyeless sockets, and lunged for the old man.

Inanna cried out. "No! Not him. Not this faithful and constant man. He is not my choice."

The demons retreated whimpering, grumbling, keening.

Walking on, Inanna was greeted by yet another figure, this one a god, who bowed low before her, his head nearly touching her feet, and again she called off the gabbling, surging demons. Again, another god came forward and humbled himself, and again Inanna stayed the clammy passion of the demon band.

As she approached the temple that had been built for her, the place where the people gathered to praise her and where she had established her bed of love and had taken Dumuzi into her an eternity before—as she approached this temple glistening in the new sun, she heard music and laughter.

Drawing nearer she was stunned to see Dumuzi himself, seated on the very bed of their passion, dressed no longer as a shepherd and keeper of goats but in royal finery. In the shadow, she stopped to hear his singing, his happy song to the harlot courtiers who languished at his feet. On her bed, *her* throne, he sat singing of his joy at Inanna's absence, at his assumption of the sovereign's crook and the seat of permanent rule.

And so Inanna of the storms, Inanna of the cyclone, Inanna of the fire and burning rock fixed Dumuzi with the eye of death. The demons lunged forward as the courtiers screamed and laid their icy fingers on the would-be king, the one who had forgotten all loyalty to his mother, all passion for his goddess mate, and dragged him away in the dust.

So every year, the rivers dry up and the land turns pallid and grey, and the people recall the death of Dumuzi. They remember in their chants and prayers how Inanna mourns with dry eyes at his annual passing, having fulfilled her promise to send a life to the Land of No Return so that she may continue to make the earth spring again into life.

And Inanna laments:

> Gone is my husband, my sweet husband.
> Gone is my love, my sweet love. . . .
> The wild bull lives no more.
> The shepherd, the wild bull lives no more.
> Dumuzi, the wild bull, lives no more.

The second of the great literate civilizations of the Near East was that of Egypt. As the Sumerian civilization emerged in the Fertile Crescent of the Tigris and Euphrates valley, Egypt grew out of the land of the Nile. And as Sumer developed cuneiform script, the Egyptians developed the form of picture-writing known as hieroglyphs by which we know their myths firsthand. By around 3500 B.C.E., they had also created one of the world's most complex and profound religious systems and a civilization that would remain essentially intact for the next three millennia. No other civilization can claim such staying power. As many scholars have suggested, an Egyptian of around 3000 B.C.E. would have felt reasonably at home in the Egypt of the Roman Empire. More than any other culture of the late Neolithic and the Bronze Age that followed, the Egyptians confronted the question of death. At the center of this confrontation were the Great Mother and the male deity as Dying God.

The Mother Goddess in Egypt took many forms. There was Nut, the sky goddess (goddess only because *sky* in Egyptian is a feminine word), who was separated from her earth-husband Geb. There was Hathor the cow goddess, and there were Maat and Ua Zit, cobra goddesses. The power behind these goddesses merged, perhaps as early as around 3500 B.C.E., into Goddess as Isis. And no mask of Goddess has ever been more powerful or longer lasting than that of Isis. She was herself the throne of Egypt on which her sons, the pharaohs, sat. She was the cow goddess, the serpent goddess, the underworld goddess, the goddess of the sacred tree of life in which, like Inanna, she sometimes sat. Her worship prevailed into the second century C.E. Most important, Isis was the fecund earth flooded and fertilized each year by the rising and falling waters that were her phallic grain-god husband Osiris.

Osiris was a Dying God. When pharaohs died, they became Osiris. This fact and that of the god's resurrection—his rebirth—at the hands of his sister-wife, make him a close relative of the Great Mother's son-lover whom we find in Sumer, Babylon, Phrygia, and elsewhere.

Osiris

He was the Mighty One, the first-born child of Geb, the Earth, and Nut, the Sky. At his birth in Thebes, a loud and mysterious voice thundered across the land, proclaiming the arrival of the Universal Lord, and all rejoiced, even Ra the Sun, though it was clear even then that Osiris and Ra could well be rivals.

And at Osiris's birth, all lamented as well, perceiving the sorrowful events that would befall him.

He grew—taller than any other, more handsome, and gentle of spirit. He was black as the river's silt and green as a field of barley, and while he embraced all things in the world, he loved nothing more than his sister Isis. When his father Geb left to dwell in the western skies, Osiris took the throne with Isis as his queen, and he sang the people of the Nile out of barbarism. Gone were the days of eating human flesh, gone was incessant war. In their stead, he taught the art of planting, the craft of tools, of making bread and wine and beer. While his sister taught women to grind corn, to spin and weave, he built villages for the people, and temples, and gave them laws, and they called him "The Good One."

Satisfied, he left Egypt in the regency of Isis and journeyed eastward. The enemy of violence, he sang the rest of the world out of barbarism, disarming all people with his divine music. On his return, he found Egypt in perfect order, thanks to the wise stewardship of his sister and queen, Isis. But the lamentations at Osiris's birth were soon to be fulfilled.

At a banquet of the gods to welcome Osiris home, his youngest brother Seth—ever a vessel of hate and jealousy—produced a large and wondrously carved coffer and said it would belong to whomever fit perfectly in it. Innocently, Osiris tried it out, and Seth and his co-conspirators leapt forward, slamming it shut, sealing it with molten lead. This done, they hurled the coffer into the Nile, whose waters carried it off into the swirls and eddies of the sea where it was lost.

Evils then plagued Egypt as Isis wailed and wandered, searching the world for her brother and husband. In due course, she received word of a marvelous scent arising from the Phoenician land of Byblos and she went there. What had happened was this.

The coffer with Osiris's body in it had floated in the currents till it fetched up on the shores of Byblos against the trunk of a sapling tamarisk tree. The tree had grown so fast that it enveloped the coffer entirely and eventually the king of Byblos had caused the tree to be cut down to serve as a support

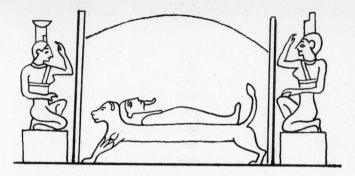

Isis and Nephthys work the resurrection spell over Osiris (Egypt, second millennium B.C.E.). (After R. T. Rundle Clark)

for his house. Once cut, the wood gave off the glorious scent and, following it to its source, Isis persuaded her queenly counterpart, Astarte, to let her carve the coffer from the tamarisk.

And so Isis brought her lover's body home and in rites of magic that are no longer known, she breathed life into Osiris's corpse sufficient for one more time of passion. Taking the form of a feathered bird of prey, a kite, Isis hovered in bliss, conceiving Osiris's son Horus. As her labor approached, she left the body and coffer of Osiris safely hidden in the reeds in the great swamp of Buto, but while she and her midwives were gone, Seth saw his chance.

He set upon the body, hacking it into fourteen pieces, which he buried here and there in the hinterlands, while the phallus he flung into the waters of the Nile, where it was devoured by crustacea and fish.

Once again, Isis and the world mourned. Now, with her young son on her hip, Isis roamed the land and discovered, one after the other, the severed pieces of her beloved consort—all but one. From secret things, she fashioned replicas of Osiris's phallus and these she planted in the lands of Egypt where, every year after the flooding of the waters, black with silt, the barley shoots rise again, green and vibrant.

And in her final act in her brother's behalf, Isis embalmed his body and conveyed on him eternal life in the underworld to the west. There, still glowing from his original embrace with Ra the sun, Osiris ruled in the land of the dead where the cosmic order prevails and sweet eternal life is given to those who are deemed worthy.

Another familiar Dying God of the Near East is the Canaanite Baal, the son of the Bull God El. He is the son-lover type to his sister Anat, who rescues him from the underworld and brings about the resurrection of nature.

Baal

Come, give them drink. Put bread on the table. Pour wine into the cups and the blood of trees into golden goblets. Ready the lamb for slaughter. Make our sacrifices to Baal and his sister, Anat, to all the gods, so the earth will reawaken, the vine regain its deep green leaves. For it was Baal, son of El, who defeated the greedy dragon of the seas and assumed dominion over the earth, and from whose palace comes the rain. . . .

Yes, Baal's palace, Baal's temple.

With the dragon senseless and defeated, Baal had looked about and saw that he, Baal, now dwelt in mud and dirt, nothing like the finery with which the dragon had been noted for. So he called out for his sister, the huntress and blood-thirsty goddess of war—Anat—and sent her to their father El to plead his case.

El said, "Of course he should have a house, but does he think I'm a common laborer? Let him build it himself."

When Baal learned he had El's permission, he sawed down the finest cedars with his lightning, and summoned the divine craftsman, Hiyon, to assemble the logs into a great temple, and to fashion for it a golden throne. Hiyon agreed, and recommended a large window be installed, but Baal panicked, thinking the dragon might revive and attack him through a window. But then he learned that, after he had subdued the dragon, Anat had come along and killed it, so he felt safe.

"Build the window," he commanded. "When it is open, I will know the earth needs rain and through it the rains will come. No more will there be floods, haphazard deluges."

Baal summoned all the gods and goddesses to celebrate his new temple and learn of his plan for the earth. But amid the merrymaking, Baal's thoughts turned to the one uninvited guest, Mot, his brother, the dark spirit of death and drought. Fearing trouble from Mot, Baal dispatched messengers to the twin peaks of the north to tell Mot that henceforth he was to confine himself to the depths below the earth and to the deserts.

Not surprisingly, Mot flew into a rage. "What?" he bellowed. "Baal wants to sit up there in the golden sun, wrapped in the garment of heaven, while I am supposed to stay here in the dark eating dirt? You go back to that pompous fool and tell him that if he won't invite me to his little party, he had better come here. I'll regale him well."

Hearing of this, Baal recoiled with fear and refused to go. Instead, he sent gifts of meat and drink. "Flatter him," he commanded the messengers, who later returned from Mot's realm with a report that Mot would have none of it. The spirit of death spurned all Baal's gifts, all his promises of fealty, and demanded his presence.

There was nothing for it, Baal concluded, so he daubed himself with ocher and decended into the world below, to partake of the feast that Mot had caused to be laid out for him. In his addled state Baal forgot that once one partakes of the food of the dead, one can no longer walk among men on the earth, and so—touching Mot's bread to his lips—he became imprisoned in the underworld.

At this, the gods and goddesses wept, but no rain fell on the earth and no green things grew. "Baal is dead!" The words reverberated around the earth and Anat was sickened with grief. Alone she wandered, tearing her flesh, her pain especially great since she had once taken the form of a heifer and born her beloved brother Baal a son, a grand bull. In her grief, she hatched a plan.

Enlisting the services of the sun, she had Baal's corpse brought up from the underworld and took it to the Mountain of the North for a funeral. Then she went to El and shrewdly persuaded him to place Baal's younger brother, hardly more than an infant, on Baal's throne. Then, her leonine eyes afire, she set out for Mot's realm where she set her dogs loose on his flocks and seized the spirit of death. She beat him with her flail, sliced him to pieces with her sickle. She set the pieces on fire, pulverized the ashes in her mill, and then buried them in the ground.

Later Anat had a dream—that the rivers' dry beds were filled with honey, and that oil poured down from the heavens. It was clearly a sign that Baal was not dead. Baal was alive. Indeed, Baal had revived on the Mountain of the North and had reclaimed his throne from his youthful brother (who was too small for the throne in any event).

But so, it seemed, had Mot revived—and he came to Baal in a towering rage. "Thanks to you I was humiliated, carved up, burnt, and put in the ground. Baal, now I will devour you!"

The battle, like that of bulls, raged long and fierce—with one gaining, then the other. Finally, helped by the sun who dazzled Mot's eyes, Baal triumphed and resumed his throne while Mot was banished forever to the underworld. The rains began again in their orderly procession and all seemed well— except to the vengeful Anat.

"Where," she demanded, "were the people, the men and women, when Baal was threatened, thought dead? They were happy enough to pay their obeisances to Baal's runt of a brother, even to Mot." And so Anat locked the gates of her house and went forth, rampaging through the land, cutting down all whom she encountered, hip-deep in the blood of revenge. Entire armies of men were slashed to pieces, the sky groaned with their cries, the ground ran with their blood.

Seeing this, Baal called Anat to him, saying "Enough." Anat paused and the sky was suddenly aflame. Lightning lit up the clouds, and thunder roared and rattled among the mountains: Baal's handiwork. Anat knew that Baal was once again and securely the king of the earth, and so she halted her rampage. Peace came, and with it, the rains, and green things grow still.

So come, give them all drink. Slaughter a fatling, and fill the golden flagons with wine.

Still another Near Eastern version of the deity as son-lover/ Dying God—one that acquired popularity as far away as Rome—was the Anatolian figure of Attis. Attis was the son-lover of the Great Goddess as the Phrygian Mountain Mother Cybele, who gives birth to Attis—the goat god—in her form as the maiden Nana. Nana had hidden in her lap the fruit of a tree that had sprung from the severed genitals of the savage Agdistis—himself a son of the Great Mother. From the seed of the fruit she conceived Attis, therefore her son-lover. The beautiful boy was brought up on a strange liquor called "he goat's milk," a bisexual term, as it were, that attains further interest in light of the one used in Anatolia to this day for the delicacy we call "Rocky Mountain Oysters," or ram's testicles. These objects are called "Ram's Eggs" (*koç yumurtasi*) in Turkey.

In the boy Attis as in the boy Horus in Egypt, the bull-child of Çatal Hüyük, and later figures such as the boy Buddha, the boy Dionysos, and the boy Jesus, we find an archetype closely associated with that of the Dying God—that of the Divine Child or Puer Aeternus. The son of the sacred nativity, produced by the Great Goddess herself in her form as mother vessel, is the eternal seed made flesh—the rising sun, the emerging plant of the spring who contains the essence of our human sense of the new beginning. He is what we potentially are, the god incarnate, the recognized Self or ego that emerges from the mysterious womb-world of the Mother. But he is also the inevitable victim, the corn god one day to be harvested, the sun that must set, the metaphor for our necessary journey back to the Mother of Being.

The advent of the Divine Child is evidenced by a miraculous conception and/or birth. Typically, he is born of a virgin. This is the myth of the Blackfoot Indian hero-god Kutoyis.

Kutoyis

Down where those two creeks meet, a man once lived with his wife and two daughters in comfort, enjoying the fruits of the land and of the hunt. But the man was getting to be old, so he was delighted when one day a young man came to his camp, a brave man and a great hunter. He gave the young man his two daughters as wives and all his wealth except for a small lodge in which he and his old wife lived.

The grateful son-in-law would hunt and share the meat with the old couple and give them skins to make robes from and to sleep on. The young man was so skilled as a hunter that before long he had managed to collect a whole herd of buffalo, which he kept under a great logjam where the creeks meet. Whenever the hunter needed some meat or a hide, he would get the old man to come with him to the logjam. The old man would stomp on the logjam, the frightened buffalo ran out, and the hunter shot one or two—never killing wastefully.

But as the months went by, the hunter stopped giving the old man any of the meat. He and his wife were hungry all the time, growing thin and weak. But the hunter still made the old man help in the hunt by stomping on the logjam, sending him home empty-handed. Lest the old man's daughters take pity on their parents, he instructed them never to give the old people anything.

This was fine with the older daughter, who had grown just as mean as her husband, but the younger daughter was different. She stole some meat and, when no one was looking, threw it into her parents' lodge. The old couple was sustained for a little while longer.

Then, on another day, the young hunter summoned the

old man to do his chore at the logjam. He did, the buffalo ran out, and the hunter shot one of them, but only wounded it. The buffalo ran off, but finally fell over dead. The old man had followed it and came to a place where the buffalo had lost a large clot of blood. Pretending to stumble and fall, the old man let his arrows fall from his quiver, and as he picked them up, he also stuffed the clot of blood into his quiver.

His son-in-law came running up. "What is that you are picking up there?" he demanded.

"Nothing. I fell down and spilled my bow and arrows."

"Curse you, you lazy old good-for-nothing," the son-in-law said, snatching the old man's bow and arrows from his quiver. "Go home."

The old man hurried back to his lodge and told his wife to put the kettle on. The old woman was pleased to think that her son-in-law had turned generous, but the old man told her that it wasn't that way. When the water reached a boil, the old man tipped his quiver over the kettle and, immediately, there came the sound of a child crying in pain.

The old couple looked in the kettle and were amazed to see a little boy in the water. They pulled him out and quickly made a cradle board for him, tying him in. Then they talked. If, they decided, their son-in-law found out it was a boy, he would kill it. But if he thought it was a girl, he would think that one day he would have another wife. So they decided to tell their daughters and their husband that they had a little girl. They named it Kutoyis, which means clot of blood.

When the hunter and his two wives came home that day, they heard an infant crying, so the hunter sent his younger wife over to see what had happened. She returned, saying that her parents had had a girl child. The hunter didn't believe it, so he sent his older wife. She came back saying the same thing, so the hunter believed her. Thinking he would some day add another wife to his lodge, he told his wives to take some pemmican over to the old people from now on so there would be plenty of milk for the growing child.

On the fourth day, the child spoke, telling the old woman to tie him in turn to each of the four lodge poles. "When I am at the fourth, I will fall out and be grown up." She did so, and

at each pole he seemed to have grown some. They tied him to
the last one, and he fell out, a grown man.

Like other versions of the Divine Child/Dying God—Horus/
Osiris, Dumuzi, and the Syrian-Greek Adonis, for instance—
the Phrygian Attis is closely associated with a tree. It is said
that he castrated himself with a harvesting sickle under a pine
tree in honor of his lover, the castrated Agdistis.

But Attis was also pursued by the Mountain Mother herself, and it was generally thought that Attis "harvested" his
genitals and died for the goddess, only to be resurrected in the
spring. In this connection, Sir James Frazer tells us that there
was a tradition in Rome that on March 22 a pine tree was cut
down and wrapped as a corpse in the temple of the Goddess
and an effigy of a youth tied to it. Blood was shed at that ritual
by the chief priest and also by the young initiate priests of the
Cybele–Attis cult, who castrated themselves in the god's
honor to assure his resurrection and general fertility.

A tree-based Dying God of northern Europe is Odin, who
enters the underworld on the traditionally shamanic eight-
legged horse and who hangs himself on a tree in order to
experience knowledge of the runes or holy mysteries. On the
tree he is the suffering god in search of a boon. He chants
these words:

> I know I hung
> on the windswept tree,
> through nine days and nights.
> I was stuck with a spear
> and given to Odin,
> myself given to myself.

All of these myths lead us inevitably to a later Divine
Child/Dying God myth that grew out of what to this stage of
the archetype was the alien patriarchal earth of Judaism. That
Jesus is an example of the deity as Divine Child and Dying
God and that he contains the genes of the ancestral shaman-

The dying Attis (Hellenistic, second century B.C.E.). (After marble relief)

trickster are suggested by several elements of the Christian myth.

In both the New Testament and the apocryphal gospels there are stories that place Jesus firmly in the position of the shaman-trickster. In the fourth-century C.E. Coptic Gospel of Thomas, we learn that as a child, in the land of his spiritual ancestor, the Grain and Underworld God Osiris, he picked some ears of corn and ate the kernels from them and that after that the field "yielded so many measures of wheat as the number of grains he had taken from it." In other apocryphal stories, the boy Jesus is depicted as having the typical trickster's childlike irresponsibility and irresistible impulse to show off his Divine Child powers. He is said to have made people go mad so as to be able to turn them sane again, to have blinded others in order to prove he could restore sight. The trickster is almost always a creator of sorts. Jesus is no exception. He turns dried salt fish into living fish, and after shocking his elders by making clay sparrows (the tricksters of creation myths often create from clay) on the Sabbath, he turns them into real sparrows. In a story from the so-called Arabic Gospel that might well remind us of the childhood tricks of another Puer Aeternus, the lord Krishna, Jesus chases some children who are afraid to play with him. When he hears them moving about in their house and their protective mother says he must be hearing goats, he turns them into goats and only turns them back at the request of Mary and Joseph. We are told in the Thomas Gospel that Jesus's teacher believed his pupil was "either a sorcerer, or a god, or an angel."

There is a distinct trickster aspect in at least one New Testament story as well. The Jesus (in Mark 11:15–17, 21–23 and Matt. 21:18–19) who curses the fig tree could just as well have been Coyote or Raven. Tricksters are beings of appetite, and in their quest to satisfy appetite, they are amoral. According to the story in question, Jesus was walking along with his disciples one day when he was suddenly hungry. Seeing a fig tree, he approached it for fruit. But when he saw that it was all leaves and no fruit, he cursed it, saying it would forever be barren, and the tree withered and died. Even the disciples were horrified by this seemingly petulant and needless act. When they asked the master for an explanation, he said he was demonstrating the power of faith, that with such faith it was possible even to tell a mountain to get up and leap into the sea.

Like all shamans, Jesus is a transformer; he turns water into wine at Cana and is the instrument by which bread and wine are turned into his own body and blood in the central ritual of Christianity. And like the shaman-trickster, he is able to transcend natural barriers; he can walk on water, cure the sick, and, most important, can raise the dead and can himself pass between the two worlds in the ultimate shamanic trick of dying on the tree and returning from the tomb. There is precedence in the Hebrew Bible for Jesus' ability to overpower death. We are told in the Book of Kings how Elisha—like most of the Old Testament prophets and most shaman-tricksters, a wandering, undomesticated man, full of the magic of his calling—revived the dead son of the Shunannite woman: ". . . he got up on the bed and lay upon the child, putting his mouth upon his mouth, his eyes upon his eyes, and his hands upon his hands" until "the flesh of the child became warm." In Elisha, the Christian reader finds the precursor to the Dying God's giving of himself so that others may live. The Dying God, like the shaman, journeys without fear into the land of death. In the Apostles Creed, we are told that Jesus, after his death, "descended into Hell." Traditionally, what Jesus did there was to harrow the dark world of Satan and to release the first parents from his clutches. The death, descent, and resurrection are a cosmic shamanic curing ceremony, reflected in the mass, in which the initiate is spiritually cured by eating the body and blood of the master shaman, now the Dying God of fertility, whose body is the "bread of life." Jesus, hanging like Attis and Odin on the cross-tree, sacrificed like Dumuzi and Osiris and all of the Dying God masks, is the new fruit on the new Tree of Knowledge and Life, the fruit available to all who would become one with the "New Adam."

There are other evident connections between Jesus and the earlier versions of the deity as Dying God. Like Dumuzi, he or his representative, the Bishop-King (bishops are "princes" of the church), is the shepherd of his flock and the "Lamb of God"—the ritual scapegoat victim whose death and resurrection are watched over by the goddess. The fact that the humble Hebrew maiden of the Nativity is turned by the folk tradition into the immaculately conceived "Mother of God" and "Queen of Heaven" is significant in light of the whole son-lover, Goddess consort, Divine Child/Dying God archetype. For the Christian, God is at once the Father-Creator, the Son-Redeemer, and the Holy Spirit–Sanctifier. In his form as the Holy Spirit, God "plants" Himself as the Son Jesus in the Mother-vessel, Mary, who after her death will reign in Heaven as His—that is, God the Father's—consort. Such subjects for Christian art as the Madonna and Child and the Pietà, in which the same beautiful "goddess" holds first the baby son and then the Dying God, are evidence of the power of the archetype.

Further elaboration of the theme in question is contained in the theological relationship indicated by the idea of the church as both "Mother church" and the "bride" of Jesus. We note in this connection the early Christian interpretation of the Song of Songs mentioned earlier. We note, too, that the actual church buildings—many of the greatest of which are named, not for the Son, but for the Mother who "contains" Him—are Christian versions of the ancient vaginal Mother caves and the kiva-like temples of the Çatal Hüyük Goddess. They are dark maternal caverns, the walls and windows of which are decorated, like the old caves, with the exploits of the shaman-king, as both Divine Child and Dying God who must be sacrificed for the fertility—albeit spiritual fertility—of the tribe. The church building, where the mysteries are celebrated, is at once the tomb of God—the altar is a place of sacrifice, a throne, and also, in appearance and in terms of the ritual, a tomb—and the womb of the Mother. The God and the initiate follower die to the old life and are reborn to a new one in the ritual of the sacrifice. So it is that the crowned victim-guardian of the cross—the symbol of the ultimate crossroad between the eternal and the temporal—seems, with arms outstretched and feet delicately posed together, to be less a victim than a Siva-like dancer-celebrant of the Great Mystery of being.

Jesus

Accounts differ, but no doubt exist that Jesus was above the humiliation and scorn heaped upon him at the end when, after a hastily contrived meeting of the elders of the religion, he was hauled in chains before Pilate, the administrator of Rome in Jerusalem.

"Are you the King of the Jews?" Pilate asked.

"So you say," Jesus said, and said no more though Pilate demanded answers to the charges leveled against him by the priests. Outside, people grew impatient, restive. It was the Passover festival when Pilate was accustomed to free whichever prisoner the people asked for.

"Shall I set free the King of the Jews?" Pilate shouted, knowing that the priests had brought Jesus to him out of envy. But the priests stirred the crowd to demand Barrabas, a thief and revolutionary accused of murder.

"What then shall I do with this man you call King of the Jews?"

And the frenzied crowd roared, "Crucify him!"

"But what crime has he committed?" Pilate demanded, and the crowd merely shrieked, "Crucify him!"

So the alien Roman turned loose Barrabas the murderer and ordered his soldiers to publicly whip Jesus and hand him over for crucifixion. He was dragged into a courtyard where other soldiers stripped him, put a purple robe over his shoulders, and jammed a crown made of thorns over his head.

"Long live the King of the Jews," they jeered, elaborately saluting him. Then they beat him with a stick, spat on him, and bowed down on their knees before him in mock obeisance. Growing tired of the mockery, they took the purple robe from him, dressed him in his own clothes and led him out into the street. Plucking a man named Simon—a Cyrenian—from the crowd to haul Jesus' cross behind him, they led the procession to Golgotha, the Place of the Skull, offering him wine and myrrh to stem the pain he would soon suffer.

But Jesus, still silent, refused and they nailed him to the cross, erecting it between two thieves each on his own cross. To Jesus' cross Pilate nailed a notice of his crime: "The King of the Jews." The soldiers then threw dice to see who would get which piece of Jesus' clothes, while the crowd looked on with ugly fascination, ridiculing him for the many claims he had become known for.

"Come down from your cross!" they taunted. "Save yourself!"

The priests joined in the mockery. "This savior of others," they jeered. "He cannot save himself! Let's see this Messiah, this King of Israel come down now, and we'll believe him." Even the thieves, hanging from their crosses beside him, took up the jeering, and Jesus forgave them.

This was at midmorning and, silent among the crowd, were many women, including Mary Magdalene, who had followed Jesus from his time in Galilee. By noon, the sixth hour of the day, a darknesss descended on Golgotha. In three hours it lifted and by some accounts Jesus cried out that he was thirsty. By yet other accounts, he called out, "My God, my God, why have you forsaken me?"

Someone came out of the crowd and held up on a stick a

sponge soaked in vinegar, pressing it to his lips, and with a loud cry, he died.

The army officer on duty, standing before the cross, had watched all this and said in amazement, "This was a righteous man. This was truly the Son of God." But Jesus was left hanging dead on the cross until a man called Joseph from Arimathea, an upstanding man of the council but secretly a believer, got Pilate's permission to take him down. He wrapped the body in a linen sheet and put it in a tomb that had been recently dug from the rock nearby, and rolled a great stone across the entrance, observed by Mary Magdalene and some other faithful women.

Two nights and a day later, after the Sabbath, the women came to anoint Jesus' body in death, wondering along the way how they would move the great boulder from his tomb. But it had been rolled back already and they panicked when, inside, they saw no body but a seated man, a stranger in a white robe, who said, "You have come looking for Jesus of Nazareth, but he is not here. He has been raised. Go tell his disciples. You will see him again, as he promised."

The women fled, too fearful to speak of this to anyone. But Jesus appeared—alive—to Mary Magdalene that day and later to two of his disciples. No one believed them. But Jesus then appeared that day to all the disciples, scolding them for their lack of faith in his promise. He ate with them, proof that he was indeed alive, not dead, and never to suffer the corruption of the flesh.

He told them to go forth and tell this good news to all in the world—that those who believe and are baptized will be saved, even able to perform miracles like picking up snakes and drinking poison without harm, like exorcising demons and healing people merely by placing their hands on the sick.

And after he spoke to the disciples, a great light filled the sky and he was taken up into the heavens to sit on the right hand of God.

The Greeks possessed a Divine Child/Dying God in the form of Dionysos, son of Zeus, born miraculously of a mortal woman, Semele (though some say his mother was Persephone). Dionysos was brought as early as the sixth century B.C.E. into the mystical fertility rituals of the Great Goddess Demeter and the disappearing goddess Persephone at Eleusis. Like his ancient sacrificial ancestors, Dionysos was a bull-god and a trickster-transformer strongly associated with sexuality and fertility. His phallus was carried in processions; the raw flesh of his animal representatives was consumed in his celebrations; and he was sometimes depicted with the grape vine emerging from his loins. His tomb was at Delphi, the sacred precinct he shared with the Great Sky God Apollo. Dionysos is the ecstatic and mystical goat-dancing inspiration that in both religion and art complements the reason and order symbolized by Apollo. And his death and resurrection ritual is the basis for the sacred choral dance drama that achieved its highest form in Greek tragedy.

The pattern of death and decay followed by germination and rebirth that is associated with Dionysos is appropriate to his role as an earth god, a nature god. Dionysos is often depicted as a newborn Divine Child nursed by Persephone herself or wild female followers called the maenads. According to some, it was as a child that he became the sacrificial victim, the Dying God. This is his many-faceted story, which includes the Orphic myth of his death, dismemberment, and resurrection.

Dionysos

He brought wine to the world and madness. He tamed the world, and they celebrated his name with blood and dismemberment, with *furor*. He was born with horns and a crown of serpents; he was murdered in infancy by his father's wife and raised as a girl. He gave tragedy to the world, too, and divine ecstasy.

He is irresistible, is he not?

Zeus plucked him as a baby from the dead body of his lover, Semele, all too mortal a woman, and the boy transformed himself into a lion, a bull, and then a serpent (in echo of the three-part year). But no disguise could long fool Hera, ever-jealous of Zeus's philandery, ever vengeful, who ordered the Titans to seize the little boy. They tore him to pieces and boiled the gobbets in a cauldron. Where his blood had fallen, a pomegranate tree grew, flowered, and fruited, its luscious scarlet body holding a promising—an irresistible—profusion of seeds.

Just so, his grandmother, Rhea, reconstituted him and brought him to life again, Zeus turning him into a goat child and giving him to fragile Persephone who had to spend half of each year in the clasp of death. She in turn gave the boy to some nymphs who reared him lovingly as a girl. But when he reached manhood, Hera saw through his effeminacy and drove him insane.

In his titanic madness, he set out across the world, bearing his sacred vines, and accompanied by Silenus and his band of satyrs, along with the maenad madwomen. To Egypt first, he went, establishing there the art of viniculture, then to Libya where he brought order to that warring land. From there, he headed for India and flayed alive the King of Damascus, who sought to block him. Once in India, he conquered all who opposed him and, divinely inspired, gave that large country its laws, its cities . . . and the grape.

Returning through Phrygia, he again encountered Rhea, his grandmother, who taught him her holy mysteries of life and rebirth, and purified him of the savagery with which he had murdered any and all his enemies. He moved on, coming to Thrace where the king, named Lycurgus, captured his entire army, Dionysos fleeing into the sea. In vengeance, Rhea drove Lycurgus into madness, in the grip of which he took his son for a tree and felled him with an axe. So horrible was this crime that all of Thrace grew barren. People began to starve and Dionysos returned from the sea to explain that Thrace would lie arid and barren until Lycurgus was executed. Immediately, his people hauled him to the top of a high mountain where horses pulled his body into pieces.

Dionysos moved on to Thebes with his band of satyrs, maenads, and a small cavalry of roistering, reprobate centaurs,

Sculpture of a dancing maenad by Scopas (Greece, fourth century
B.C.E.).

wine flagons ever-replenishing—a drunken ecstasy. In the
midst of these revels, Dionysos asked the local women to join
in, and the ground shook with their insane release from the
shackles of decorum.

Outraged, the King of Thebes, named Pentheus, arrested
Dionysos and the howling, reveling maenads, who soon escaped to continue the revels in the mountains. And Dionysos,

slick and persuasive, talked Pentheus into shedding just some of his self-control and going to the mountain to watch the orgy. But in their blind ecstasy, their wine-enriched frenzy, the women of Thebes seized Pentheus and ripped him into pieces. Indeed, his very mother, Agave, was the one who unwittingly wrenched Pentheus's head from his shoulders.

Thenceforward, Dionysos swept throughout Greece and the remainder of the world, establishing his divinity among all people, even among the straight-laced Romans, who called him Bacchus. Wherever he went he spread joy, terror, a delicious pandemonium, and people—especially women—sang his praises and danced, and drank, and made love, and tore goats to pieces in his honor. The people could not get enough of him and held aloft fetishes that proclaimed phallic marvels.

With the world addicted to him, he ascended into heaven and sat at the right hand of Zeus, having first persuaded gentle Hestia to give up her place among the Twelve Great Ones and seek peace somewhere among men, thus avoiding the constant bickering of Olympus.

And the bickering continued. For Dionysos, upon reflection, descended into the underworld where he bribed his once-foster mother, Persephone, to release the wraith of his true mother, Semele. He installed her (with the alias of Thyone) in heaven to be with him forever, safe finally from the vengeance of the bitch-goddess Hera, who fumed in helpless silence, all her plans having gone sourly awry.

In ancient Mexico, a particularly powerful god among the Toltecs and Aztecs was Quetzalcoatl, the "Feathered Serpent." Serpents, of course, are always fertility and resurrection symbols, since they slough off their old skins in favor of new ones. Quetzalcoatl was a creator of cities and the founder of agriculture and the arts. In one of his more remarkable acts, he "dies" in order to revive humanity.

Quetzalcoatl

Snake-bird.

> Plumed serpent.
> God of the wind, the master craftsman of life.
> The civilizer, creator, patron of all the known arts.

This was Quetzalcoatl, god, founding king, and priest who taught men to sing of himself/herself: She of the star-studded dress, he who lights up all, mistress and lord of our flesh, who brings life to the world, maize and cotton, who sustains the earth.

Quetzalcoatl lived in a house of jade and quetzal plumes, the very home of the sun itself, and all of the succession of kings of the Toltecs, the master craftsmen, acted just as Quetzalcoatl did in the beginning. Indeed, they became Quetzalcoatl, seeking through prayer and meditation to see with a clarity of vision the two faces of the dual god they had come to be. They—he—presided over the Golden Age, the fabled time before the new ones came from the northeast—the necromancers bent on destruction.

One of these was Tezcatlipoca, a treacherous one, who people saw entering the city one day, his bear face blackened and painted with stripes. They did not see him seduce the niece of Quetzalcoatl but soon became aware of the lawlessness and vice that resulted. The canny Tezcatlipoca danced with bells on his ankles and sang during a festival, and people lost their heads, imitating him, congregating in revelry on a bridge. But the bridge collapsed under their weight and they perished in the river. Others died, suffocated, when they looked upon the magical puppet dancing in the necromancer's hand.

The people who remained stoned him to death, but his body stank so horribly that some died. The rest dragged him out of town, hoping that was an end to it, but Tezcatlipoca revived and returned and entered the palace of the great god-king Quetzalcoatl.

There, he played a trick on the god, producing drink, and a mirror.

"I have come," the sorcerer said, "to show you your body."

"Welcome," Quetzalcoatl said. "Please explain yourself."

"Look in the mirror. That is you." And Quetzalcoatl saw himself, bearded, with a long and homely face, and he was frightened. If my people were to see me, they too would be frightened, he thought, and decided he would have to leave. For four days he lay in a stone box and, finally feeling ill, he rose up, sang a long and sad song, promising one day to return from the East, and left, accompanied by bright-colored birds.

When he reached the great sea to the East, some say, he went across the divine waters in a boat, one day to sail back. But that is not what happened.

Upon reaching the shore, he donned his green mask of jade and his multicolored plumes and, thus adorned, he set fire to himself. The ashes of the plumed serpent were immediately raised up, along with a great flight of birds of all hues, tinting the eastern sky. This is why he came to be known also as the Lord of the Dawn. After his death, the dawn did not come for four days, while Quetzalcoatl descended into the underworld. But again he arose in the morning, enthroned in the morning sky as a star.

Before appearing as the morning star, while still among the dead, Quetzalcoatl went to the Lord of the Dead and pointed out that the earth was not inhabited. He announced that he would take the bones that lay around in the Kingdom of the Dead and put them on earth. He gathered them up in two bundles—one the bones of a man, the other of a woman—and carried them upward. Once on earth, he ground them up and cast them on the ground and threw upon them some blood from his penis. Thus, it is said, did the earth come to be peopled.

And people—now the Aztecs—remembered Quetzalcoatl and recalled his promise to return. So they kept a watch on the easternmost shore of the land. But in his absence, they welcomed other gods, including Texcatlipoca, the treacherous necromancer who was also the sun—giver of warmth for the

Quetzacoatl (Mexico, ca. 1000 C.E.). (After photograph of figure in the Brooklyn Museum)

crops, but also the edgy, unpredictable bestower of drought. To appease him, the Aztecs offered him the hearts torn from the chests of the handsomest prisoners of war.

One day, the sentries on the eastern perimeter of the land saw someone coming across the sea, glittering and shining. They ran to their emperor and pontiff, Montezuma, and

gladly announced that Quetzalcoatl had returned. Montezuma
sent presents including a snake mask adorned with turquoise
and the plumes of the quetzal bird, an emblem of the god.

Of course, it was not Quetzalcoatl but the Spaniard named
Cortés. Within a year, Cortés had destroyed the great city
where people still remembered Quetzalcoatl. He sacked the
great city and burned it, even setting fire to the aviaries that
graced every home with color and song. The songs of the birds
were silenced; the story ended, but people remain who still
wonder if perhaps Quetzalcoatl will one day make good his
promise and come home.

Quetzalcoatl's primary city was ancient Tollán. When the
forces of evil overthrew his city, he was forced to flee, but it
was always said that one day he would return. The myth was
so strong that when Cortés arrived in Tenochtitlán, Montezuma himself believed, tragically for his people, that Quetzalcoatl had returned.

So it is that Jesus, Dionysos, Quetzalcoatl, Attis, Osiris,
Odin, Faro, Dumuzi, Baal, the bear of the Cherokee Bear
Man myth, the corn wrestler-angel of the Ojibway myth, and
the Trois Frères shaman/animal master/trickster are all part of
the same biography. It is God's biography and in a sense ours,
as we move from—but never wholly shed—the stage of the
egotistical, childish but creative servant of Earth to the understanding that growth requires the sacrifice of the old in favor of
the new communally oriented self.

III

The Marriage and Divorce of the Archetype: Sky God and Earth Mate

Lovers (Mesopotamia, ca. 2000 B.C.E.). (After clay plaque in the Louvre)

In the course of his movement from trickster and sacrificial victim to Supreme Being, the male divinity was faced with the powerful barrier of goddess power. Yet, as the people depended increasingly on male strength for the plow and for herding, and as the cult of the male "seed" in animal husbandry developed, the male divinity became increasingly significant.

Eventually, as his power grew, God was seen as the equal to, the true mate, of Goddess, who was still associated with Earth. In this role God was often equated with the sky itself with little attempt on the part of his worshippers to personalize him or to provide him with a mythology of his own. In ancient Sumer, Anu, the relatively abstract god of the sky (Anu means "sky"), lived in the "Sky House" and the stars were his army. In Vedic India, Dyaus is a personification of the Sky, who in union with Prthivi (Earth) is literally Sky–Earth. The name *Dyaus* in Sanskrit is obviously related to other Indo-European words for the male divinity, such as *Dios, Dieus, Zeus,* and *Deus,* all of which are rooted in Sanskrit terms meaning "bright sky." Dyaus was supplanted in early Vedic times by the god Varuna, who with Mitra was considered, among other things, god of the sky. The Mitra–Varuna figures in pre-Zoroastrian ancient Persia were Ahura Mazda (who later developed more complex characteristics), sometimes associated with the day sky, and Mithra, the night sky. It was said that Ahura Mazda wore the "vault of Heaven."

The idea of God as the sky is especially present in African mythologies. He is known as Sonhaskan (the Sky Being) or Nyankupon (the Thundering One), Ngai (Rain), Olurun (Sky Owner)—and there are many other names. To say, as the Tschwis people do, that Nyankupon has come is to say it is thundering or raining. Among some of the Bantu people, the Supreme Being is Leza, and to say Leza is falling means it is raining. Among the Ewes, the name of the High God Mawu means "to cover" and it is the sky that covers his face. For some of the Masais, the Supreme Being, Ngai, means rain.

Whatever he is called, in many African cultures, God withdrew from human concerns a long time ago and is characterized primarily by his aloofness. As such he is not much worshipped. "God made man," say the Bantus, "but then he left him alone"; the same concept is repeated by the Fang people, the Negrilloes, the Hottentots, and many others. It seems fair to suggest that among many of the world's most ancient cultures, the sky-god was at first defined by the very fact of his unreachableness and mysteriousness—his unknowableness. It is not difficult for us to imagine that when Stone Age people gazed at the sky they sensed the vastness of existence and perhaps the possibility of what we call the "spiritual" or "transcendent" experience. From very early times, the male divinity can perhaps be said to have stood as a catalyst for and goal of the human mind's need to expand its consciousness beyond the world of the Earth Mother, the world of the cycles of death-defined existence. Survival depended on the worship of the Great Mother, but the human thirst for something beyond the physical was perhaps somewhat satisfied by her ever-present yet boundless mate.

A pervasive theme in the Sky God–Earth Mother marriage is the separation of Earth and Sky, usually by their own offspring. The resentment of parental sexuality is not, it seems confined to the child of Freudian mythology. But a more important reason for the separation would seem to be found in an essential requirement of creation itself. The union of Sky and Earth is suffocating to the creative drive; it represents a primordial unity which in its essential indeterminacy is a kind of chaos. A description of this state is found at the beginning of the oldest extant creation epic, the Babylonian *Enuma Elish:*

> When on high there was no name for the sky
> And Earth itself had no name,
> Only Apsu, the progenitor existed
> And the bearer of all, the primordial Tiamat,
> their waters in union as one being.

In their androgynous undifferentiated union, the primordial couple represent a passive, even entropic state.

The separation of the pair leaves room between them for the processes of differentiation on which creation—the development of cosmos out of chaos—depends. To put it another way, with the separation of the world parents we achieve creative duality, the two sticks necessary for the friction that can create fire.

The most famous example of these world parent separation myths is the Egyptian one of Geb and Nut (Earth and Sky), in which the traditional roles of God as Sky and Goddess as Earth are reversed (because of the gender of the words in question in the Egyptian language). Often the great beings are held apart by the god Shu (air).

Geb and Nut

At one point, Ra the Sun governed all that was, but he grew old. His bones grew silvery, his hair the blue of sapphire, and the people of the time noted this change and began to think evil thoughts. Perhaps, they thought, it was an opportune time to rise up in revolt against Ra.

Of course Ra knew what they were thinking and decided to slaughter them all, but he called together some lesser gods for a consultation. These suggested, instead, that Ra first send forth his Eye, his fearful Eye, to command the respect of the people. Ra promptly did this and the people all fled in terror into the desert but remained surly and rebellious. Then the gods suggested that Ra's Eye go forth after them and slaughter them. As a result, most people died.

By now Ra was disgusted with these noisome ingrates. He decided to step down as governor of all things, and chaos returned for a time. One of the gods, Geb, was appointed god of the earth, and Nut became goddess of heaven, but confusion continued because Nut lay directly upon Geb, her spouse.

Geb and Nut. (Egypt, ca. 1000 B.C.E.). (After photograph of Papyrus of Tanienu)

Realizing that this would not do, the gods persuaded Shu, the air, to shove himself between the two. Once he had done so, Nut was raised upward, higher and higher, balancing on her extended arms and legs, and earth became separated from heaven. Nut, in the form of a great cow, then lofted all the gods in their boats into the heavens, counted them, and made them the stars. One of these was the Sun itself which travels daily across Nut's belly, while at night the other stars twinkle there.

Meanwhile Geb, now separated from his spouse, took on the active governorship of earth. He became the prince of the gods of earth, the most potent of all, with power over all of the earth's heritage, the lives of its inhabitants, and their possessions.

We are also told in the Indian *Rig-Veda* that the creator god pushed Heaven off Earth to bring order out of chaos. And the Minyong people of northeastern India tell the story of how Sedi the Earth Mother and Milo the Sky had to be separated so that their offspring could have room to live.

Sedi and Milo

Sedi is the earth, a woman. Milo is the sky, a man.

These two came together early in the beginning of things and clung to each other in a grand and passionate embrace. At the time, there were beings called the Wiyus—both men and animals—and they found that they were going to be crushed between the two cosmic lovers. In haste, they held a meeting called a Kebang to see how they might save themselves. It was agreed that one of the greatest of the Wiyus, named Sedi-Diyor, should try to save them, and he caught hold of Milo the sky and thrashed him so hard that he fled up into the heavens, leaving Sedi the earth behind.

The Wiyus found now that they had room, and they breathed easily. And as the sky fled upward, Sedi gave birth to two daughters. It was out of the experiences of these two daughters that light would eventually come to the earth—day and night, and all that is thus brought forth.

The Greek version of the world parent separation myth was told by Hesiod in his *Theogony*. Here Earth is the Great Goddess Gaia and Sky is Uranos (Ouranos). Uranos "covered" Gaia constantly until she and her children devised a means of removing him from her.

Gaia and Uranos

In the beginning there was Chaos, the gaping openness of space.

Yet out of Chaos there emerged Gaia, the deep-breasted earth, and soon afterward Eros, the power of attraction whose influence would always thereafter be felt in Gaia's creations.

At this time, night and day were born from Chaos, and Gaia's first creative act was to give birth to Uranos (Ouranos), the sky crowned with the stars, a son she made her equal in grandeur. Covered entirely by her son, she put forth the mountains and the sea, and then she slept. The universe had thus been created, waiting only to be peopled with plants and animals, gods and people.

Uranos looked down affectionately on Gaia from above the mountains and showered rain down on her, where it trickled and coursed into her most secret clefts. And from these arose the trees, grasses, flowers, the beasts and, gathering in her hollows, the lakes.

The first semi-human beings to be sired by Uranos upon Gaia were the Cyclopes, wild and rebellious sons with but one eye apiece. Dismayed with them, Uranos cast them into the underworld far away.

Gaia, who by then had already given birth as well to the divine race of Titans, seven strong, sought revenge on her son/ husband and persuaded the seven Titans to attack their father. Led by the youngest, Cronus, whom she armed with a sickle made of flint, they set upon Uranos while he slept. Cronus seized his father's genitals in his left hand and the flint sickle swept down. Then Cronus threw the genitals and the sickle into the sea as Uranos lay dying. But some of the blood fell on Gaia and she gave birth to the Furies, bent on taking vengeance on those who lie or kill their fathers. Knowing this, Cronus who was made sovereign, took to swallowing any children born to him. And it was only after his son, Zeus, escaped this fate, that the gods of Olympus came into being.

Some early Roman writings and archeological finds indicate the existence of an ancient Aryan-Celtic myth of the primal pair being separated by their children, who castrate their father and make the sky out of his skull and the sea out of his blood. In this myth, the castrating son becomes god of the underworld and the good children become the new gods of sky and earth.

In the Maori myth of Rangi (Sky) and Papa (Earth), we find once again the idea that the unity of the primal parents was suffocating and that creation depended upon their separation.

Rangi and Papa

All living things sprang from the union of Rangi and Papa, Heaven and Earth—Rangi and Papa who cleaved together in the darkness that existed from the first division of time until the thousandth. For the beings that sprang forth, then, there was no light but only the darkness between their parents in this vast space of time.

The offspring of Rangi and Papa prayed, singing of the darkness, of the light they only dreamed about. They sang of the seeking, the searching in chaos. They wondered what to do: they could either slay their parents in hopes of achieving light, or they could try to wrench them apart. One of the six beings—who were all brothers—called for their parents' death, but another, the god of the forests and trees counseled that rending them apart would be better.

"Let the sky become a stranger to us but the earth remain near, a nursing mother."

All the brothers agreed, except for the god of wind and storm, who was called Tawhirima-tea and who feared that his own kingdom would thus be destroyed. Nevertheless, the other brothers undertook the job of rending apart their parents who still clung together in the dark.

First the god of cultivated human food struggled and failed, then the god of fish and reptiles. He was followed by the god of wild human food. At last, Tane-mahuta, god of the forests and their inhabitants tried—but in vain. But he struggled on, with his head against Papa the earth, and his feet against Rangi the sky. With a mighty effort, finally, he wrenched them apart and they groaned and cried out in pain.

"Why do you commit this terrible crime," they shrieked, but Tane-mahuta kept pushing, and heaven and earth were torn away from each other, and suddenly, plainly for all to see, there was darkness . . . and there was light. And in the light could be seen the great multitude of human beings that Rangi and Papa had begotten and who had lain so long, unknown and unseen between them.

But Tawhirima-tea, god of the storm, was beset with evil thoughts and these he brooded into clouds of all kinds and whirlwinds and squalls, and these he unleashed from all quarters, wildly thundering down on the forests and the sea. Trees were uprooted, left lying there to become loathsome rot, and the seas churned and raged.

The father of the fish and the father of the reptiles consulted, to think of how to save themselves, and eventually the reptiles fled inland while the fish fled into the sea. The two fathers were enraged at each other and fought. The forest god made canoes and hooks from the trees so his children could conquer the fish, and the sea raged against them, overturning their canoes, flooding their houses, sweeping away living things into the great ocean.

At the same time, Tawhirima-tea raged on, attacking the two gods of human food—cultivated and wild—who hid in inaccessible valleys and glens. Finally, one of the original six sons of Rangi and Papa, Tu-matauenga, rose up against the god of the storm. He—Tu-matauenga, or fierce man, who had wanted to kill his parents in the first place—stood firmly in defiance on the breast of earth, and Rangi and the god of storms fell back. The earth was tranquil.

Next, Tu-matauenga subdued each of his other brothers in turn, to make the world safe for the growing numbers of his progeny and to feed them. Of all the five other sons of Rangi and Papa, only Tawhirima-tea of the storms could not be vanquished and turned into food. He still attacks to this day, seeking to destroy humanity and its sustenance by both sea and land.

The Micronesian people of the Gilbert Islands have a similar animistic creation myth in which the separated Sky and Earth become the new creation.

Nareau

Here in the world of the great ocean there is an eternal one. It is Nareau, who commanded the sand and the water to join and produce offspring.

One of the many offspring of the sand and water was Nareau the Younger, and he called upon all the others to rise up and live. But they could not rise up because the sky was so heavy on the earth.

So Nareau the Younger killed his father and made from his eyes the sun and the moon. He placed his father's spine upright on the island of Samoa and this became the world tree, and all human beings were born of this tree.

An ancient Chinese creation myth, also with animistic characteristics associated with the separation of Heaven and Earth, is that of the Yin–Yang giant Phan Ku.

Phan Ku

At first there was only chaos, contained in an unimaginably huge egg. The chaos was Yin–Yang—a mixture of female–male, cold–heat, light–dark, wet–dry, active–passive—and within this Yin–Yang was Phan Ku. Phan Ku, in this earliest moment, was not anything yet, but suddenly it broke forth from the egg as a giant, and it began separating chaos into the many opposites, including the earth and the sky.

Phan Ku stood between the sky and earth and every day for 18,000 years Phan Ku grew ten feet. The sky was thus raised ten feet each day, and the earth itself grew by ten feet. That is why heaven and earth are now separated by 90,000 li, or 30,000 miles.

Phan Ku himself was covered with hair, and he had horns that sprang from his head, tusks from his mouth. Taking a great chisel and a huge mallet, he carved out the mountains, the valleys, the rivers, even the oceans. During his 18,000 years, he also made the sun, the moon, and the stars, and taught the people what they know. All the world, both heaven and earth, was suffused by Yin and Yang, the great principles that had existed even in the original chaos.

After 18,000 years, Phan Ku died. His skull became the top of the sky, his breath the wind, his voice thunder, his legs and arms the four directions, his flesh the soil, his blood the rivers. And the fleas that lived in his hair, some people say, became us human beings.

Everything that is is Phan Ku. Everything that is Phan Ku is Yin–Yang.

But the death of Phan Ku left a vacuum in the world, and in the vacuum pain and sin arose and were able to flourish.

The Diegueno Indians of southern California tell how the creator used the power of tobacco to separate the primal oneness.

Tu-chai-pai

It is told that when Tu-chai-pai, the Creator, made the world, it was cramped and uncomfortable. Tu-chai-pai had made the earth as a female and, at this early time, she was little more than a shallow lake filled with rushes. At the same time, Tu-chai-pai had made the sky male, and it came down over the earth and the Creator and his brother were stuck uncomfortably in between.

So Tu-chai-pai took some tobacco in his hands and rubbed it and blew on it three times. The sky rose a bit over the earth.

Then he and his brother both blew on the tobacco and said certain magic words, and the sky went all the way up.

This was a great improvement, and the brothers set about making the four directions, and the hills, valleys, and lakes. Knowing that they wanted to create people, they made forests of wood that the people would need for building things. And then, when everything was in place, Tu-chai-pai announced that it was time to make the people.

He took up some mud and made the Indians first, then the Mexicans. He made both men and women, but it was more difficult to make women. He told all the people they would not have to die but, instead, they would have to walk all the time. He gave them sleep, which would let them be still and rest through the night, and said that they should walk toward the light in the east.

After a long journey eastward, the people found the light of the sun and they were happy. Now, Tu-chai-pai's brother made the moon, and the two brothers told the people that when the moon got small and seemed to die, they must run races, and it would grow large again.

The people did this, and Tu-chai-pai's work was done. The world as we know it had come into being.

But of course, Tu-chai-pai kept on thinking for a long time.

Another story in which smoke, if not tobacco, plays a role in the separation is one told by the Krachi people of Togo in Africa.

Wulbari

In the very beginning of things, Wulbari (who is heaven) lived on top of Asase Ya, who is Mother-Earth.

Mankind lived between them, but there was very little room between Wulbari and Asase Ya. The people squirmed in discomfort, and this was very annoying to Wulbari.

One old woman, they say, kept hitting Wulbari with her pestle as she ground her maize, and the smoke from her cooking fire bothered his eyes. Some say that men sometimes wiped their dirty hands on Wulbari, which was also very irritating, and it is rumored that one old woman took to cutting bits of Wulbari off to flavor her soup.

Wulbari soon grew impatient with all these annoyances so he left and went up aloft where he is today.

The Zunis of the American Southwest say Earth-Mother herself pushed away Sky-Father so that their offspring might be able to see and know one thing from another.

Earth-Mother and Sky-Father

In the fourfold womb of the world, all terrestrial life was conceived from the lying together of the Earth-Mother and Sky-Father upon the world waters. Soon, Earth-Mother grew large with so great a number of progeny. She pushed Sky-Father away from her and began to sink into the world waters, fearing that evil might befall her offstpring, just as mothers always fear for their firstborn before they come forth.

Unnerved by this foreboding, she kept her offspring unborn within her and discussed her fears with Sky-Father. Together, they wondered how, even in the light of the Sun, these offspring would know one place for another. Changeable as are all surpassing beings, like smoke in the breeze, the couple took the form of a man and a woman.

Suddenly a great bowl filled with water appeared near at hand to Earth-Mother and she realized that each place in the world would be surrounded by mountains like the rim of the bowl. She spat in the water and, as foam formed, she said, "Look! It is from my bosom that they will find sustenance."

She blew her warm breath over the foam and some lifted upward, shattering, sending down mist and spray in great abundance. "So," Earth-Mother said. "Just so will clouds form at the rim of the world where the great waters are and be borne by the breath of the surpassing beings until your cold breath makes them shed, falling downward—the waters of life falling into my lap where our children will nestle and thrive, finding warmth in spite of your coldness."

"Wait," said Sky-Father and he spread his hand over the bowl, setting in its crevices what looked like yellow corngrains gleaming in the dark of the early dawn of the world. He took seven of them up between his thumb and fingers and said, "When the Sun is not nearby and all is dark in the world, our children will be guided by these lights which will tell them the regions of space. And just as these grains shine up from the water to light the sky, so will numberless seedlings like them spring up from your bosom when my waters touch them, and our children will be fed.

In this way, and in many others, Earth-Mother and Sky-Father talked and provided for their progeny, the people and other creatures of the world.

The Nigerian Binis have an unusual separation myth in which the Sky removed himself from Earth because of the outrageous behavior of human beings. Yet, in a sense, it is because of that removal that people became productive.

The Bini Sky

In the very long-ago, the sky lay close to the earth. Those were times when men had no need to cultivate the ground and grow things. Instead, whenever they grew hungry, they had only to cut off a piece of the sky and eat it.

This did not upset the sky, but it made the sky angry when the people took to cutting off more than they could eat and tossing what was left over onto the rubbish pile. This was simply no place for a piece of the sky and so the sky told men that they had to be more careful about what they cut off or the sky would go away—far away.

Now everyone was greatly chastened and they paid careful attention to the sky's warning and threat. But one day a greedy woman cut a huge piece off the sky. She ate and ate but finally could eat no more. In a panic, she called her husband and he set to eating the rest of the piece, but he couldn't finish it either. They called on everyone in the village to help but, in the end, there was still plenty left over. There was nothing to do but throw it on the rubbish pile.

Infuriated, the sky rose up far away from the earth, far beyond the people's grasp. So, from that time until now, people have had to work for their living.

The separation, for all of it positive characteristics, seems to suggest a movement toward the dominace of an Iron Age (beginning ca. 1250 B.C.E.) male divinity who would stand alone above creation and control the passive Earth. The separation of the creator from creation would result in a disregard for the sacredness of Goddess, the Earth. But it is important to remember that at the transitional stage God as sky-god was himself primarily passive. Although often thought to be all-knowing and all-seeing, a sky-god characteristic that would predominate in later stages of God's development, at this stage he took no particular interest in human affairs. Earth was clearly still the precinct of his Goddess mate, whose worship by human societies bent on earthly survival was much more important than his.

Eventually, God would awaken to his own potential for power in the form of the warrior god who entered the Indian subcontinent, old Europe, and the Middle East with the invaders from the Aryan north during the late Neolithic and Iron ages. From his home in the sky the male divinity would discover new power in a more particularized role. Once the co-creator with Earth, he would name himself as sole creator of the world. But first he would have to apply the techniques of the warrior to defeat the Earth power of his mate.

Goddess power was mysterious; its source was in the depths of the Earth itself—the world represented by the sacred cave-temples and the mysteries of germination. God power was there for all to see in the sun's rays and in the thunder's sound, the lightning's fire and the sheer immensity of the sky. Through the army of the stars and the great eye of the sun, the sky-god could command all things. As male power on earth, embodied in the invading warriors, took precedence over the female power of the agricultural mysteries, it was inevitable that a mythological struggle would take place to reflect that loss of balance once expressed in the androgynous union of the primordial chaos and later more specifically in the creative separation of Earth and Sky as primordial World Parents. In the mysteries of Earth power, the Aryans would find a perversion of the power that could be measured by success at arms. The mysteries of the Earth were somehow a threat to male dominance.

The struggle that resulted was a terrible one, one that led to a lasting and somehow basic division between male and female. Female power was no longer seen primarily as a nurturing force but as an abberation from the frightening depths, one that must be conquered or destroyed. Where Goddess had once been all things, she now was associated with darkness and chaos; she was at best the moon as opposed to the sun. Enter the golden Aryan warrior god, the representation of ego and the male's view of himself as the bringer of order, reason, and light, who longs to disarm the dark ambiguity of the unconscious depths. Unlike the old sky-god, the new figure takes an active role in human affairs and demands worship. He is no longer content to leave earth and humanity in the control of what he sees now as the monster Mother. This is the god, for instance, of the Iron Age cultures of Mesopotamia—the Babylonians and Assyrians whose warriors and sometimes brutal practices stood in contrast to the gentler ways of the earlier Sumerians. This was a war god who would influence the god of the Hebrews and the gods of Greece and Rome. He was a god whose power was measured by the ability of his followers—Hammurabi, David, Achilles—to conquer others. He was the god who is still with us to the extent that we find virtue in conquest, whether of nature, the "weaker" gender, or another ethnic or religious group.

One of the earliest representations of the new version of male divinity is the Babylonian Marduk. Marduk's temple, the great ziggurat, was the central edifice in the ancient city of Babylon, symbolizing the ascendancy of the new Aryan war god, the sun god, and male power in society. Mythologically, Marduk achieved his position of dominance by defeating the World Mother, Tiamat, the primeval waters who had become a monstrous serpent—a forerunner of the dragon slain by other heroes in later myths.

In the Babylonian creation epic, the *Enuma Elish*, from which this myth is taken, Marduk not only defeats the primeval Mother, but takes on the creative role of separating Heaven and Earth, thus making a giant step toward the sky-god's emergence into the all-powerful Creator God.

Marduk (I)

"The Old Hag has made the Worm! She has loosed the Dragon, the Female Monsters, the Mad Dog, Scorpion Man, the howling storm! She loathes us all, our mother Tiamat. Her horrid new brood, with venom in their veins, plot furiously against us, snarling!"

Marduk standing supreme on the primal waters (second millennium B.C.E.). (After Charles Long)

Thus did the gods, the children of Tiamat the Sea, bewail the traitorous malevolence of their mother as they met not for the first time in the Hall of the Synod to ponder their destiny in the early inchoate world.

"With their pitiless weapons, these monsters she has hatched, these eleven unflinching monsters, are led by Kingu whom she has taken as husband and made supreme. On Kingu's chest she has fastened the bronze tables of fate. The horrid monsters now surge up form the raging sea, from the blind Old Hag, and none of us has been able to confront her."

Then Marduk stood up, among the most recent of their lineage, and said, "If I must be the avenger, if I must go kill Tiamat and save all your lives, then you must give me supreme precedence over all. My decrees shall be unalterable, never to be annulled, and my creation will extend to the very ends of the earth. I shall decide the nature of the world."

The assembled gods agreed. If Marduk could avenge them, he was king of the entire universe. They gave him the scepter, helped him onto the throne, and bestowed on him matchless weapons of war. But Marduk made his own weapon—a bow, strung with an arrow, and a mace. Then he armed himself with a net and with an atrocious wind, the hurricane, and, burning with a terrifying light as if from within, he set forth with the winds towering behind him.

He approached the Deep, Tiamat, wallowing in blind fury, and she spat out her bitter disdain. "Upstart," she roared. "Do you imagine yourself to be so great?"

"You have mothered war itself," Marduk accused. "You've given that pathetic bungler, Kingu, the rank of a leader, and you have abused the gods. Stand up, then, and we will fight it out, you and me."

Tiamat shrieked, seized with hate, trembling with malevolence, but Marduk hurled his net and caught her in it. He unleashed the atrocious wind in her face and she lunged, mouth agape, to swallow him. But Marduk drove the wind into her mouth so that she could not close it, and the wind filled her belly to bursting. Next, Marduk shot an arrow that pierced her stomach and split her heart. She sank, dying, moaning in agony, and Marduk stood astride her.

The monsters of Tiamat cowered and fled but soon found themselves enmeshed in the wise Marduk's net, then flung—along with Kingu—into the infernal realms of the underworld. Turning back to the corpse of Tiamat, Marduk smashed her skull with his mace and severed her arteries so that her blood flowed to the ends of the earth. While the gods applauded, he cut the body in two, constructing from one half the arc of the sky, from the other the solid earth.

He stretched out the immensity of the heavenly firmament and made palaces for the gods, each in its constellation. He marked out the limits of the year, giving the sun instructions to complete its annual cycle, and provided the moon with a bright jewel with which to do his nocturnal work. He scooped up the spittle from Tiamat's dead mouth and tossed it high, to become the clouds, the spindrift of the oceans, the wet wind, and the life-giving rain.

And with the world formed, Marduk set out to create in it something that would make the gods rejoice. He brought forth the rivers and plants and wild animals and then created mankind. And the hearts of the gods leapt to see this creation.

There are many examples in world mythology of the enlightened god's destroying of the older chaotic elements of original creation, though these forces are not necessarily female. In Canaan, Baal, sky-god of thunder and lightning, struggles against the Water God Yam, whose life is spared only through the pleading of the Mother Goddess Asherah. Although Yam is not female, it is of interest to note that it is Baal who brings fertility to earth, whereas Yam seems to wish only to flood it into entropic passivity. Yam thus plays the role of the Babylonian Tiamat.

The Athabascan people of North America tell of the culture hero who detooths and thus conquers the monstrous "Vagina Girls," walking vulvas who devour the males they crave.

In India there was a story in which the River Goddess Ganga was subdued by the male power of Siva. There was also the story of the ancient feminine earth monster Danu or sometimes Vritra and her defeat at the hands of the male Indra, the representative of the Aryan culture that had invaded the Indus valley.

In Greece, the great sun god of light and reason, Apollo, achieves his ascendancy by defeating the female dragon-earth monster Python.

Apollo

As was so often the case, the problem arose in part because of Hera's infernal jealousy, her inability to understand the responsibilities that call a supreme lord, such as her consort Zeus, to action.

The idea that Zeus should give birth to a daughter, Athena, from his very head, that he should bring into the world this glorious, bright-eyed paragon of wisdom *without* Hera but totally by himself . . . it struck Hera as even more dishonorable than the bastard children Zeus sired on a variety of nymphs and lesser goddesses. So, in her taut-faced rage to which the gods had become accustomed, Hera bemoaned her disgrace and announced her intent to have a son of her own, conceived and born without male intervention of any kind.

Forswearing Zeus's bed, she went off with a heart full of anger and prayed to the Titans in the underworld, to the Earth and to Heaven for a child stronger than Zeus, just as Zeus was stronger than his father Kronos. The Earth was moved and life stirred in Hera's womb. The goddess confined herself to her own temples for a full year and gave birth, to her utter dismay, to a dreaded and wicked thing unlike god or man, a misshapen serpent certain to bring sorrow to mankind.

So Hera took it and gave it to the she-dragon, big and fat, who had long meant bloody misery to both men and their sheep. The dragon raised this serpent as her own and, together, almost as one malevolent being, they did plenty of terrible things to the tribes of mankind.

It was at a time when the she-dragon and her inseparable Python were dwelling near a spring at Crisa, below the shoulder of the mountain called Parnassus, when Apollo came there. He, the god of light, the archer god, had come to this peaceful and quiet place to establish a temple of beauty, an oracle where mankind could receive from him the truth. He had laid out the foundations and a stone base for the temple when the she-dragon rose up in terrible anger from her subterranean den.

Undismayed, Apollo loosed a great arrow at her. She fell to

the ground, torn with pain, gasping, rolling around, shrieking. Among the trees in the wood she thrashed and breathed up blood and life left her.

"Rot there," Apollo commanded. "No longer will you bring monstrous evil to humans. Instead they will bring perfect sacrifices to this place, and you and your malevolence will rot here in the black earth in the piercing light of the bright sun."

Thus did Apollo establish his altar in this place, where people could come for all times to see the light and learn the truth from the Delphic priestess called by some the Pythonness.

Throughout the world were stories of solar heroes who represented the values of the new male power and who defeated such monster remnants of the old goddess as the Gorgons, the Chimera, the Sphinx, and any number of dragon-mothers who have descendants in figures such as Grendel's mother in the Anglo-Icelandic tale of Beowulf and the more subtle *femmes fatales* whether Pandora, Eve, or the Hollywood "vamp"— "monsters" who consantly threaten the noble male and his sense of right and reason in the myth and literature of both the East and the West from the Iron Age on.

IV

The Dominance of the Archetype: King God

Zeus as Thunder God (Dodona, Greece, fifth century B.C.E.). (After bronze figure)

When we think of the chief gods of world mythology as opposed to those that we associate with the word *religion*, we tend to bring to mind figures such as the Greek Zeus, the Roman Jupiter, the Norse Odin. These are masks of the storm and war god who has separated Heaven and Earth and harnessed the great power of the sky. Often he is the sun, itself the ultimate symbol of cosmic order—the regular, predictable, unmysterious, linear passing of time and the seasons, light and darkness. He sits enthroned "on high" surrounded, mandala-like, by planetary pantheons of lesser gods and humankind below, the symbol of hierarchy. The representative of the god on earth is the Indo-European sun king who also sits at the center of a sacred circle outlined by the defensive walls of new male-centered cities.

The sun god cult is ubiquitous in the ancient world. It seems fair to say that sun worship is at the basis of our sense of Supreme Being. In Mesopotamia, Marduk, the source of the sacred kingship and the slayer of the female monster Tiamat, is associated with the sun which brings light out of darkness, order out of chaos with each daily rising. In this, he resembles the Greek Sun God Apollo, the destroyer of Python, and the Indian Supreme solar deity Indra, who defeats the darkness, which is the monstrous night serpent Vritra. In Egypt, the Supreme Being was for a time Amen-Ra, the Sun God, whose rule over the sky and orderly passage justified the sacred kingship itself. With the development of the Osiris cult, the pharaoh in death was the setting sun, the Dying God Osiris, reborn as that god's son, the rising Sun God Horus. Horus was conceived in the Delta swamps where Isis revived the dead Osiris sufficiently to bring forth his seed. Horus would later avenge his father's murder by defeating the monstrous Seth.

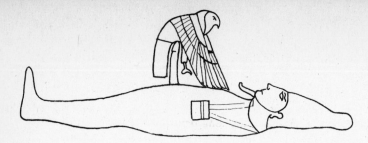

Isis as a kite conceiving Horus on the dead but aroused Osiris (Egypt, second millennium B.C.E.). (After Abydos temple painting)

Horus as the sun rising from the dead Osiris (Egypt, second millennium B.C.E.). (After R. T. Rundle Clark)

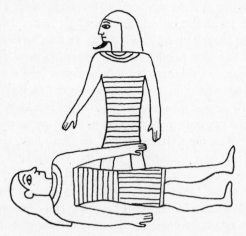

Horus arising from Osiris (Egypt, second millennium B.C.E.). (After R. T. Rundle Clark)

Horus

How great the raging storms, how loud the keening wails of mourning, how dark the long days after Osiris died and the murderer Seth and his henchman spread their fetid tyranny over a world without hope. So tight were the chains of despair that the gods dwelled in terror and panic and even Atum, the Master of Destiny, retired to his boat in the sky, turning his back on the doings of the world and hoping that someone else might emerge to take control of things.

There was a stirring—a quickening—in the womb of Isis, who awoke with a start in the realization that she was pregnant with the seed of her beloved brother Osiris, resurrected so briefly, hovered over so lovingly, before his final passage.

Heart rejoicing, Isis slept again and dreamed a prophecy: that she had formed the body of a god within her who would rule over this land, the son of him who earlier presided, and that he would come to inherit the patrimony of Geb and slay his father's murderer, the evil Seth. Though this god was still an unformed embryo within her, Isis enjoined the pantheon of gods to protect him for he would be their master, lord of all the mighty.

And in the dream, Atum called forth to the gods to protect the unborn seed of Osiris in Isis's womb.

When the unborn child's time came, Isis came to Atum's divine court and said, "Make way! It is a falcon within me that I am giving birth to."

With that, a falcon emerged and Atum called upon the followers of Osiris to worship it. Isis asked that another seat be made for her newborn son-falcon among the followers of Ra, the Sun, as they sit in his eternal boat and that her son be admitted to the company of eternity's guides.

But the falcon, who would be named Horus, sought his own destiny and soared aloft into the sky, beyond the realms reached by the original bird-soul, well beyond the stars, those gods of Nut who dwell in the constellations. He flew, indeed, beyond the created universe and alit upon the easternmost ramparts of forever where the world ends.

From there, Horus called out his name—Horus the great Falcon. "I have taken my place beyond the powers of Seth who killed my father, I have done what no other god could do. I have brought light and the eternal ways into the twilight of morning. I am Horus and my domain stretches far beyond that of gods and men. I am Horus, son of Isis."

And indeed, out of the dark and confusion of the time of Seth, out of the long reign of despair, there came this herald of the new world, a great age aborning, a transcendent time of light.

In India, Surya, another anthropomorphized version of the sun, is he who sees all things. He is the "eye of heaven" or the eye of the great sky-gods Varuna and Mitra. In Norse mythology, too, the sun is the eye of the chief god, Odin.

Among the Incas of Peru, Viracocha was the sun, who emerged from Lake Titicaca to create the world. The emperor of the Incas—"The Inca"—reigned as the god's earthly self. Inca architecture and city planning was such that the people could have a clear view of the east, where the god rose each day. The huge Sun Temple in Cuzco dominated everything around it; it was the "Place of Gold," surrounded by lesser temples to the Moon and other deities who formed the Sun's entourage. The temple gates were arranged so that the Sun shone on various parts of a great central disk within at particular seasons of the year. The Sun, as always, was the ultimate embodiment of the life principle; he was also the source of order and the regular passing of time.

Viracocha

Viracocha was one of his names, the Sun, but he was not so easily definable. He was beyond all comprehension. He may, as the ancients say, have arisen in the very beginning from Lake Titicaca, and surely he did make the stars, the planets, the moon—and set them on their orderly paths in the sky. Surely, indeed, he created everything, even the people.

It was, we think, like this.

On a great hill there were three caves called the Tavern of the Dawn. And from the central cave one day emerged four brothers. They were Ayar-manco, the leader; Ayar-auco, the warrior; Ayar-cachi, the salty one; and Ayar-oco, the peppery one. With them came their sister wives—Mama-occlo, the pure one; Mama-huaco, the fighter; Mama-ipagora; and Mama Rawa. These brothers and sisters were free to go where they wished, but the Sun told them to carry with them a golden rod which was to be struck in the ground wherever they came to rest. "Teach the people to be kind and good," Viracocha told them, "and I will provide warmth and light."

Led by Ayar-manco, the brothers and their sister-wives traveled here and there, inventing the world we live in now. Along the way, it became clear that Ayar-cachi, the salty one, was too strong by far, so the others tricked him into entering a cave. Then they rolled a mammoth rock in front of it to lock him in, and this is called the Traitor's Stone, not far from Cuzco.

In fact, it was near the valley of Cuzco (which didn't exist then of course) that the group saw an idol that was obviously a sacred thing. Awed, Ayar-oco, the peppery one, touched it and immediately turned to stone, the very stone now called Huanacauri on a hill of the same name.

So the two remaining brothers and the four sisters rested and, as he had been instructed, Ayar-manco thrust his golden rod into the ground. To his amazement, it sank deep into the earth—clearly a sign. He ordered his brother Ayar-auco, the warrior, to stand on a cairn and proclaim this the site of a grand new city to be built, a city where the people would come to live. Ayar-auco climbed on the cairn and, himself, became a stone—the cornerstone for the city to be.

Then Ayar-manco built Cuzco, high in the mountains. He built the House of the Sun, a grand temple to Viracocha, and with Mama-occlo, gave birth to the first Inca and *his* sister who was also his queen. To gather the people and preach the rule of the sun, Viracocha, the Inca, went north while his queen went south—both dressed in wondrous shiny clothes, hanging with brilliant ornaments of metal and feathers. The people who were scattered here and there in the mountains and valleys were greatly impressed and learned all the lessons the Inca and his queen had to teach them, and they gathered in the grand new city of Cuzco. The Inca himself founded the northern part of the city, his queen the southern part, and so all Inca cities were organized, representing the male and the female, and all the other opposite things that are so useful and provide so much pleasure.

In the Sun Temples of ancient Mexico there were rites similar to those of the Incas. The Toltec-Aztec people were "Sun Children." Their association of the old god Camaxtlui with the "sun of the past" and the god-king Quetzalcoatl with the "sun of the present" is not unlike the Osiris–Horus association in Egypt.

The prominence of the sun metaphor to depict the Supreme Being expresses the sense of the sun as the essence of life, as the *sine qua non* of existence. The sun is the instrument by which the powers of night and darkness are overcome, the source of light and warmth without which there can be no life.

With the rise of the solar male to supremacy over Goddess, the dominance of the trickster, the "spirit of disorder, the enemy of boundaries" (Kerenyi, in Radin, *Trickster*, 185), is over and there is no longer any need for the male god to sacrifice himself to the goddess. The battles with the female Earth power are behind him; his goddesses are destroyed, as in the case of Tiamat or Danu. Or they are relatively tamed wives like Siva's Parvati and Odin's Frigg. Or they are de-feminized like the armored Athena or the virgin huntress Artemis. Sometimes, as in the case of the Greek Hera, the wife of Zeus, they are reduced to the role of jealous shrew. The point is that God has become King of Heaven, just as the human male had become the central ordering force in the earthly patriarchies, where a "man's home" was "his castle" in which the woman was a possession. In her capacity as a wife, she served him, betrayed him, or was betrayed by him. As a daughter, she was married for a price.

In the early stages of his ascendancy, the new King God still had clear connections with his earlier role as a fertilizer of the Earth Mother. His mark was often thunder and rain; in addition to being the sun god, he was a weather god, the bull or ram of heaven who impregnated the Earth Mother at will from above. As father and king, the sky-god of the patriarchal Aryans must be, above all, virile, the carrier of the sacred seed of life. The emphasis on the male seed is clear in the myths of separation of Heaven and Earth in which the severed male genitals of the old gods like Uranos become the source of new life even as the new sky-gods take power. But the fecundity of the old gods was indiscriminate, whereas that of the new gods is part of a controlled and conscious process.

A creation myth of the Chukchee Eskimos of northeastern Siberia tells how Raven, traditionally a trickster, also acts as a fecundating sky-god, competing with his life-giving wife in a male–female struggle marked on his part by a motivation that Freud might have called "vulva envy."

Raven (II)

Raven came into being of his own accord at the very beginning of things, and he dwelled with his wife in a small and cramped space enclosed in a vast gray void. It was not long before Raven's wife began to complain to him about being bored.

"There's nothing to do, nothing to see, there's nothing. It's boring." This went on for a long time until one day Raven's wife, having said yet again that life was boring in this tiny space with nothing to occupy her, asked Raven why he didn't make some amusement for her. "Why don't you create an earth or something?" she whined.

"I can't," Raven said, not wanting to be bothered.

"Well," said his wife with an imperious snort. "In that case, *I* will make something." With that, she lay down and went to sleep, while Raven watched, wondering what was up.

As she slept, his wife began to lose her feathers and at the same time grew fat, her belly swelling up until it seemed like it would burst. Even without stirring or waking up, she released two absolutely similar beings from her body—twin somethings. Like the mother now, they had no feathers. Instead they were just little writhing lumps of skin. Raven was disgusted and said "Ugh, how awful."

The little twin somethings with no feathers heard this and woke up their mother. "What's that?" they squalled.

"It's your father."

The twins laughed and laughed, pointing at his feathers, squealing about how harsh his voice was. "How awful," they mimicked, croaking, "How awful." Then Raven's wife told them to stop fooling around, it was rude, and they did.

After that, Raven's wife seemed satisfied. She had created what *she* called humans, after all, and this made Raven uneasy. He decided that he had to create something too. So he flew to the Benevolent Ones—Dawn, Sunset, Evening, and all the others who had always been out there but weren't enough to satisfy his wife's cravings for amusement. He asked them to help him imagine what he should create, but they had no advice for him.

Raven shrugged and flew on until, down below him, he saw some strange-looking beings sitting around in space. He joined them and they said they were the seeds of the new people, but they couldn't fulfill their destiny without an earth. Could Raven create one?

Well, Raven had been thinking about that ever since his wife asked him to create an earth, which he hadn't then wanted to do. But now he did, and he had an idea. He asked one of the man-seeds to come with him and he soared up into the sky. Once aloft, he got a sublime grin on his face and began to relieve himself. He shat and he pissed and his mighty droppings fell to the ground and became the mountains, val-

leys, rivers, oceans, lakes. Raven shat and pissed the earth
into existence.

But the man-seed clinging to him asked what people
would eat, so Raven redoubled his efforts and the beginnings
of plants and animals rained down on earth like heavenly hail.
The man-seed asked to be put down among all this largesse,
and before long there were many men flourishing on this new
earth. But there were no women—not that the men noticed
any absence.

But little Spider Woman appeared and began making
women. The men were fascinated with these new things but
didn't know what to do with them. With a special twinkle in
his eye, Raven said, "Let me teach you about these things."

And he began to teach the men about copulation.

"You see," Raven would say. "This is what you do. Now
this one over here is a little different so you do it this way
. . . and, now, this one. . . ."

In India the great fecundator of the Vedic period was Indra,
whose immediate antecedent was Parjanya, god of typhoons.
Indra was called World Bull—that is, world fertilizer. It was he
who made seeds active, who brought rain, and who gave
women the power to reproduce. And, of course, Indra is the
god of thunderbolts and, as we have noted, a solar god. In
Greece and Rome, the King Gods Zeus and Jupiter played
similar roles. As power in Greece passed from Uranos and
Kronos to the fecundating Zeus, so in ancient Sumer it had
passed from the old earth spouse Anu to the storm god Enlil.

It is to be noted that God as fecundator in his new warrior
mask was no gentle lover of the Great Mother. He planted his
seed as he willed, and his sowing was often characterized by
the violence that marked his other activities. As many scholars
have pointed out, numerous cultures have long associated the
bull with God, the bull being a symbol both of fertility and
power. Perhaps the best known of the bull-god tales is that of
Zeus and Europa.

Zeus

So here on the Olympian heights sits Zeus in all his majesty, heaven's very father on the throne of the gods, world-shaker and commander of the fork of lightning, and his eye alights with a gleam—the ever-renewing, never-changing gleam of lust—on the tender luscious form of a cowherd of Tyre, a girl as juicy as a melon, as intoxicating as the promise embodied in a grape: innocent Europa.

So Zeus, staring greedily across the great spaces at this haunting apparition, signals to his son Hermes.

"Here, Hermes, you wily executor of my wishes, see over there that royal herd of cattle grazing in mountain pastures? Glide over there on your swift heels, my boy, and drive those cows to the seashore. There's a good lad."

In a trice, Hermes is in the mountains and the herd turns, heading for the great blue horizon of the dark sea, but Zeus cares not about cattle, His eye is on the rising, falling haunches of Europa. Abandoning his throne and scepter, Zeus is all at once among the cattle on the mountain, a lowing bull ambling handsomely through the deep green grass, his hide as white as the new snow before the south wind brings melting rain. The muscles of his great neck swell, all silky, a grand dewlap sways below, and jewel-like pearly horns rise toward the sky. In his shining dark orbs of eyes there is a kindly serenity.

Europa is transfixed by so beautiful a creature and plucks up some wildflowers which she holds out daintily to his soft white lips. He frolicks and cavorts in playfulness, delighting her, and she rests her hand on his white flank, her pet bull. She mounts his back.

So the great Bull God Zeus sets forth on spurious hooves into the sea, taking his prize into the open water while she, suddenly fearful, clings to his pearly horns. Fetching up on the shores of Crete, Zeus, father of all, reveals himself before her, abruptly turns into an eagle, and takes her under a willow tree just inland from the sandy strand.

That is how things were with Zeus. He had his passions

Zeus and Europa (Greece, ca. fifth century B.C.E.). (After photograph of vase painting)

and they needed to be assuaged. Of course, there was a great hue and cry: Europa's father sent her brother Cadmus off to find Europa and he traveled all around the world, had many adventures, but—as far as Zeus was concerned—it signified nothing. The great god had his pleasure and Europa gave him three sons, and Zeus went on to other pressing matters.

There had been earlier versions of the bull-god as rapist. Enlil, the great fecundator of the Sumerians, raped the beautiful young Nilil, who protested that her "lips" were too small to copulate or to kiss. Sometimes creation itself is the result of a fecundating act that breaks other human taboos. The *Rig-Veda* in India tells of the first god, later identified as Prajapati, coupling with his own daughter at the beginning.

Prajapati (I)

He was in the very act of union, the satisfaction of his over-
weening desire for the young girl, his daughter, splayed out
beneath him, and he pulled back. He withdrew his eager
phallus which had already entered into her depths, and some
of his seed was shed upon the back of the earth, the womb of
good deeds. So, with some of the father's seed in the daughter's womb, yet some of it spilt on the earth during their
union, and the benevolent deities created out of this sacred
speech along with the Protector of Ceremony . . . and the
god of fire made from this seed the excellent youths, the great
ones, even as the father satisfied his lust for his daughter
. . . oh, heaven is the father, the engenderer, and the
mother is the wide earth, the womb outstretched between the
bowls . . . yes, the hunter shot the arrow, the god satisfied
his lust . . . his lust.

Perhaps the ultimate fecundating myth is that of the Egyptian
high solar god Atum (Re) as told in the Pyramid Texts of
around 2500 B.C.E., in which the supreme deity creates the
first beings, Shu and Tefnut, without the assistance of a feminine component—that is, by masturbation. Pyramid Section
527 tells us that Atum "in Heliopolis created by taking his
organ in hand and achieving the pleasure of ejaculation out of
which came male and female—Shu and Tefnut." It should be
noted, however, that this myth cannot simply be seen as an
example of the male god's dominance over the female. In a
sense, Atum looks forward to the great androgynous He/She
that would become the concept of Brahman in India. And as
popular as the creation by masturbation story was in Egypt,
Atum was eventually seen as a male whose masturbating hand
became the goddess Iusas.

In any case, fecundity was only one aspect of the new male
supreme deity, the solar warrior King God. The primary as-

pect was the idea of order that emerged from the rise of male power and the suppression of female power during and after the Aryan invasions. The priority of order is certainly related to the development of new cities such as those of the cultures of Mesopotamia, Egypt, the Indus valley, and later Greece and Central and South America. Where the magic and mysteries of agriculture had been central to the old Mother-dominated cultures, the emergence of the Father God and his earthly representative, the Sacred King, paralleled the development of the urban cultures that grew up in connection with primarily male activities such as the mining of metals, architecture, the making of weapons and tools, defense, and technology in general. Elements of the new patriarchy exist, in fact, as early as the early fourth millennium B.C.E. in Sumer, suggesting that the male-oriented social system and religion might have supplanted the Mother Right even without the Aryan invasions from the north. The old Goddess culture had taken its power from the very qualities that had become anathema to the new activities—qualities to which we apply terms such as "the mysteries" and "the depths." More important to the new increasingly urban and technological societies was visible power and what they saw as the light of reason and a certain predictability. The complex city-states must vie with each other in commerce and war, not in mysterious powers of the Earth. It was no longer necessary for everyone in society to be concerned with the growing of crops or the domestication of animals. With the new technologies, whole groups of people, not occupied with animal husbandry and agriculture, could specialize in technologies and crafts that, as people increasingly depended on them, would lead to the accumulation of wealth and male power.

It might be suggested that the emergence of the Sacred King and the all-powerful Father God, with both of whom concepts such as discipline, authority, justice, and reason were associated, came naturally with the desire of the male to protect his newly gained prestige and property. So it was that the high god was a storm god, a war god, a rain god, and a sun god, and his earthly viceroy was at once priest, judge, and head warrior. Power was being consolidated. God controlled all things, and his "eye," the sun, could penetrate any depths. God was now prepared to consolidate all deities within himself and to emerge fully as sole lord and creator of the universe, the ultimate Father God. In so doing, he would complete his usurpation of the role of the Great Mother of pre-Aryan times; like her, he would become the source of and essence of all being.

V

The Theologizing of the Archetype: The Creator God

The Egyptian god Ptah throwing the cosmic egg on a potter's wheel (second millennium B.C.E.). (After Lyn Constable-Maxwell and Wallis Budge)

Many forces conspired to bring about the next stage in the biography of God. As late as the Iron Age (ca. 1250–100 B.C.E.) it was still common for king gods to be, like Zeus and Ra, leaders of large and complex family units called pantheons. Responsibilities for various aspects of life could be delegated to beings within these units. Zeus was king, but his brothers Hades and Poseidon were in charge of the underworld and the sea, Apollo was the god of light and reason, and Athena embodied wisdom. But in the Iron Age, there was a strong movement in much of the world toward a consolidation of godly power, a movement that reflected, on the one hand, the political, social, and military priorities of a violent age of war—priorities centered in hierarchy and conquest—and, on the other hand, a pride in mental powers as opposed to those of the Earth mysteries. These were powers associated more with the male than the female; they were dramatically articulated in the growing use of written language and in the technology that resulted in not only new weaponry, but monumental architecture and great cities. As warriors and builders, the men of the Iron Age put a high priority on the efficiency that seemed to follow from political absolutism and hierarchy. Such priorities were naturally enough expressed not only in family life and politics but in religion. This was the age, for instance, of the Hebrew god Yahweh or Elohim, the ruler, and, more important, the creator of the universe.

That God—not only in his form as Yahweh—should come to be known primarily as the creator is significant. In many cultures, he would claim through his male priesthoods to be the source of all being, who himself had always existed. Such a god had no need of a father and mother, a queen, brothers and sisters, or even children. As the creator, he was the logical result of the usurpation by earlier divine masks of essential life-giving powers. His immediate arthetypal ancestors were the sky-god fecundators of a depersonalized earth who denied the old female source of fertility and attributed that power to themselves, the sun gods, whose passage through the skies proclaimed light, order, and reason and whose very being, like that of the sun, was the essence of existence.

There had long been signs of monotheistic power or at least of single-god dominance. In Mesopotamia, the Sumerian Enlil and later the Babylonian Marduk took what was almost supreme creative power. In Egypt, there had always been a strong tendency toward a kind of Creator God monotheism. We have seen that Atum claimed to have created the universe from himself in a masturbatory act. As early as 3000 B.C.E., the Egyptian High God as Ptah was the supreme creator, the source of even the other gods. And the pharoah Ahknaten, in around 1300 B.C.E., attempted to establish a Sun God monotheism.

In Vedic India, the god Indra was tempted by supreme power and had to be reminded by less ostentatious but infinitely stronger powers of his proper place in the scheme of things. But even in this reminder, there is a hint of a Supreme Divine Power that is the source of all that is.

Indra

The dragon's reign was over. Indra, the god, had thrown his thunderbolt and the dragon was dead—she, the limbless cloud serpent, the horrid being who had held the world's waters in her belly. Now the juices of earth flowed again, the rivers streamed in the sunlight, and the monsters retreated to the underworld.

All the divine ones sang of Indra their savior, and he set out to rebuild the city of the gods with an unrivaled splendor, fitting for the very king of the gods—Indra himself. He gave his orders to the god of arts and crafts, Vishvakarmans, who soon produced a marvelous residence, but Indra's visions of grandeur always outpaced the builder's ability, and he began to despair. He appealed to Brahma, the universal spirit of creation, for help, and Brahma in turn went to Visnu, the Supreme Being, who agreed to help the despairing builder.

The next day a boy with the staff and garb of a pilgrim appeared at Indra's gate, asking to see the king. A gentle, radiant boy with eyes shining with the luster of wisdom, he was ushered into Indra's presence and lavishly fed with honey, fruits, and milk.

Then the boy said, "I have heard of the marvelous palace you are building and I've come to ask how long it will take to complete." He smiled. "No other Indra has ever been able to complete so grand a palace as the one you have envisioned."

Indra was amused by the boy's pretension that he had known other Indras, that other Indras had existed. "How many Indras do you suppose there were before me?" he asked with gentle sarcasm.

The boy began by naming some and then explained, "King of the Gods, I have known them all. I have seen them come and go in the endless cycle of things where everything is destroyed, every atom dissolving into the pure waters of eternity, the incomprehensible darkness, only to be reborn by Brahma with the support of the enduring supreme being, Visnu. There have been more Indras than grains of sand on earth or drops of rain."

At this point, a column of ants four yards across began to march through Indra's palace, and the boy laughed, an abrupt peal of amusement, followed by a silence.

Nervously, Indra asked what was so funny. "Who are you, disguised here as a boy?"

"I laughed because of the ants. They bear a secret that lies buried in the wisdom of the ages—a secret that destroys the proud."

Indra begged to hear the secret, and finally the boy relented.

"Each ant," he said, "each ant in the great procession was once an Indra whose noble and reverent deeds elevated him to the rank of King of the Gods. But each, through many births into this world, has become again an ant. See the army of former Indras, now crawling in dumb obedience across your floor. Wicked deeds have cast them into the sloughs of pain, sorrow, to become vermin, deformed from their former beauty. Look closely, Indra. They are monsters."

The boy continued, as Indra realized his own insignificance. "Death masters all. Good and evil succeed each other in the endless cycles of time, and the wise attach themselves to neither good nor evil. They seek more than merely joy or the bliss of redemption. Even Brahmas come and go with each eyeblink of Visnu. This world is as fragile as a dream."

With that, the boy vanished, and Indra decided to become a hermit and seek the eternal presence of Visnu, to pass on his responsibilities and the splendor of his palace to his son. But his wife, Sachi, intervened, asking the Lord of Magic Wisdom to reason with her husband.

The Lord of Magic Wisdom, called Brihaspati, explained the virtues of the spiritual life but also the virtues of the secular. He taught Indra the art of governing the world and of being always a wooer, and thus was Indra the king cured of his ambition and learned the wisdom of playing his proper role in the endless turning of the wheel of life.

The sense that a real Supreme Being existed before all things and created the universe is not limited, then, to the monotheistic Abrahamic religions (Judaism, Christianity, and Islam) or their direct ancestors. It is a recurrent theme in the human dream that is world mythology. Several versions of the creator stand out in that mythology. The most common is the god who creates *ex nihilo* (from nothing). Sometimes he creates the world by thinking or, as in the case of the Australian Aborigines, by "dreaming" it or, more often, as in the case of the Abrahamic versions, by speaking it. The "word" of god was his *logos*—his order, his essence—perhaps reflecting the fact that language had become an increasingly useful tool since the development of cuneiform script in Sumer in the late Neolithic period. The connection between thought and creation and language and creation is logical when we consider the fact that it is through thought and language that we humans make creation at large conscious of itself. The mytho-logic behind this role for humanity is the nearly universal idea that in the original creation the Supreme Being made humankind in his image. Humans would be minigods, minicreators who would maintain contact with the ultimate mystery through their prayers and sacred texts, words containing the mysterious power of the original creative act.

In this myth of ancient India, Prajapati is the creator, whose greatness was embodied in his words.

Prajapati (II)

At the beginning there was only Prajapati and, in due course, he wondered how he might produce some progeny. He practiced being an ascetic until he was exhausted, and then from his mouth he produced Agni, the first of the gods. Agni is an eater of food, and so must all who know him be eaters of food.

Agni's mouth gaped for food and Prajapati grew scared. "Here is this food-eater I have created from myself, and there is no food for him but me. But," he reassured himself, "Agni will not eat of me." Speech was Prajapati's greatness and speech went forth from him. He rubbed his hands together to produce an offering, and it came in the form of clarified butter. But the butter was mixed with the hair from his hands (the palms of hands are no longer with hair as a result of this) so he poured it into the fire. "Svaha," he told the fire, "Burn and drink this." And from this oblation, or burning, came the plants of the earth.

Prajapati rubbed his hands together again and obtained another offering of butter, perfect butter, and he paused.

"Should I offer this or keep it?" he thought to himself. But then, in speech, in his greatness, he offered it, saying "Svaha."

And with that, the sun warmed, the wind blew, and Agni—who was in truth Death—turned away while Prajapati's progeny came into the world, and Prajapati was saved from Death who was about to devour him.

So if you know this, you can save yourself from Death. When you die and are put in the fire, you will be reborn from the fire just as once you were born from your mother and father. For the fire consumes only your body, after all.

The universe of the Maori people of the South Pacific was spoken into being by the god Io, a figure possibly influenced by the god of the Christian missionaries. As always, the creator exists before creation but in a state of nondifferentiation. Cosmos is born out of chaos only when by thought and word he creates boundaries that differentiate and make form.

Io

Io, who is the hidden face, lived in the breathing space of the immense universe when all was darkness—only darkness, surrounded by water, water everywhere. Dawn never glimmered, nothing was clear. There was no light. Io needed to act and so he spoke, telling the darkness to become a darkness containing light.

Light appeared immediately.

Then to keep busy, Io told the light to become a light that contained darkness.

Darkness immediately enveloped all.

Seeing the power of his words, Io began to chant:

> Let one darkness be above me
> And another darkness below.
> Let darkness extend to Tupua
> and darkness extend to Tawhito.
> Let the darkness be overcome and vanish.
> Let there be one light above me

Wood carving of Io. (After photograph in Charles Long)

And one light below.
Let the light extend to Tupua
and let the light extend to Tawhito.
Let the light reign over all,
A bright light.

A great light now prevailed in the universe, and Io gazed at the enveloping waters, chanting:

Let the waters of Tai-kama be separate.
Let heaven arise.

Io watched as the sky came into being above him. And again he spoke:

Bring forth Tupua-horo-nuku.

Immediately the pulsing earth stretched out before him.

So today, my good friends, we use these ancient and original sayings, this wisdom, these words that brought existence from the void, and heaven, and the tides, and the pulsing, life-giving earth.

We speak them when we implant a child in the womb; we speak when we ritually enlighten the mind and the body; we speak them when we ritually talk of important things—war, baptism, ancestors. For the universe was implanted by Io's words and produced light. For all rituals to enlighten and cheer the spirit, Io's words overcome the darkness. And by Io's words, the continuing birth of the universe goes forward. And so, my friends, we chant Io's words to this day.

The Mayan Indians in their holy book, the *Popol Vuh*, tell of the great god who is the "heart of Heaven" and who inspires his lesser companions to think creation into being.

The Heart of Heaven

Darkness, silence. Nothing moved in the perpetual night.

In the water, distantly surrounded by light, were the Creator, and Tepeu and Gucumatz, the forefathers. They were sages, thinkers.

And there was the sky, and the god of all, the Heart of Heaven, who goes by that name.

Then, into the silence came the word from the Heart of Heaven. Tepeu and Gucumantz came together, unseeing in the darkness, and they talked and deliberated, their words and thoughts becoming one. It became clear that when dawn broke, mankind would have to appear, so they planned the creation, the growth of trees and plants, and the birth of life itself, and the arrival of mankind.

It was the Heart of Heaven who arranged this in the original darkness.

Perhaps the ultimate *ex nihilo* creation story belongs to the Uitoto Indians of Colombia in South America.

Nainema

Listen carefully. Put down the tools and the cares of today, and listen carefully for this is how it is. This is where we are.

First there was Nainema, but Nainema was nothing but a vision, an illusion. There wasn't anything else. But the vision which was Nainema affected itself deeply.

So Nainema took this vision which was himself unto himself and meditated. He held the vision by the thread of a dream and looked into it, searching . . . for what?

He found nothing in the vision so he searched within it

again, tying the empty vision to the dream-thread with a magical glue. Then he took the vision, this phantasm, and methodically trampled the bottom of it until the earth he dreamed was enough for him to sit upon.

Now, sitting, holding on to the illusion, he spat a stream of saliva and the forests came into being and grew. Nainema then lay down on the earth and envisioned a sky above it, which also came into being.

Then, gazing intently at himself—he, the one who was the story itself—created this story for us to hear.

Now do you understand?

Nearly all of the creation myths of the patriarchies that replaced the old Mother Right convey the sense of a Father God who creates by the power of his mind rather than by way of the mysteries of the earth. As has been indicated, he is a god clearly influenced by the new male-dominated arts, crafts, and technologies of the late Neolithic and Bronze and Iron ages. God has become a manipulator of materials who molds nature to fit the designs of his own imagination. Nature itself—once the basis of Goddess power—is sacred only when he makes it so by claiming it as his own. Another popular version of the creation myth, therefore, involves the craftsman creator, or *deus faber*. These are gods whose work is analogous to particular arts and crafts, such as pottery, weaving, architecture, and carpentry.

Among the *deus faber* creations is a particularly sophisticated one told by the Dogon people of Mali. The god in question is Amma—a sound meaning "One God." Amma marked his creation by a series of sacred words or epiphanies associated with particular crafts. Activities such as pottery and weaving, were sacred tasks by means of which Amma became articulate among his people; pottery and weaving were his language, much as agriculture had been the language of the ancient Earth Goddess.

Amma

Amma, the one God, threw some pellets of earth into space
and they became the stars. But to create the sun and the
moon, Amma first had to invent the art of pottery. For the sun
is, in a sense, a pot fired to white heat and surrounded with
eight turns of a copper spiral. The moon is much the same, but
surrounded with white copper.

Then, as he had done with the stars, Amma took a lump of
clay, squeezed it, and threw it. It fell in the north and spread
southward, extended east and west as well, like the limbs of a
foetus. This feminine body lay flat, face up. Its sexual organ
was an anthill, its clitoris a termite mound.

Now Amma was lonely and deeply desired to have intercourse with this enticing creature, in hopes of producing other
creatures. As Amma approached, however, the termite mound
rose up in masculine erectness, barring Amma's passage. It
was as strong as Amma's own organ and intercourse was impos-
sible. But all-powerful Amma cut down the termite mound
and had intercourse with the earth, and this, it turned out, was
the first time the order of the universe was breached.

From this union, there arose a single being, the jackal who
is the symbol of Amma's difficulties.

Amma continued to have intercourse with the earth, and
now that the termite mound had been excised, it went on
normally. Water which is the divine seed entered the earth
and brought about the birth of twins—human from the head to
the loins, and serpents from there down. They were green,
with red human eyes and the serpent's forked tongue. They
gleamed like water, and soft green hair—an early notion of
vegetation—covered them.

Called the Nummo, these twin spirits were born perfect
from a perfect union. At birth, they possessed speech, which
all living beings need. They were also the essence of Amma,
made from his seed which is the life-force of the world: water.
The twins are themselves water, present in the seas, rivers,
lakes, and storms. We drink them.

The Nummo went to heaven to receive their father's orders and, looking down, they noticed that their mother, the earth, was naked. Also, she was without speech. So the Nummo took sheafs of fibers from the plants they had already planted in heaven, and took them down to the earth, where they wove them into two strands—one for the front, one for the back.

The fibers fell in coils; they were the essence of Nummo, of motion, a helical line that undulates to infinity. The Nummo spoke and from their mouths came a warm mist that is speech. The moisture of speech was imparted into the coiled fringes of the skirt. So the earth was given order. It had speech, the first language. It was a primitive language to be sure, but it was enough for the great works that would take place to begin all things.

The Yuki Indians of northern California have a creator who makes the world using the analogy of house building.

Taiko-mol

First was foam floating here and there across the fog-shrouded waters in the dark.

At some point long, long ago, a voice came from the foam and then Taiko-mol appeared, with eagle feathers on his head. He was the creator, and he rode on the moving foam and sang things into creation.

First, he made a rope and laid it out north-to-south. Then, in the dark, he walked along its length, coiling it as he went. As he coiled the rope, it left behind the new, fresh earth. But soon the water overwhelmed it. Three more times Taiko-mol did the same thing, laying out a rope and coiling it to create a new earth, and three more times the waters overran the earth.

Taiko-mol decided there had to be a better way. He made four stone posts and anchored them to the earth in each of the four directions. To the posts he attached lines and stretched them out across the world, by way of a plan. Then he spoke the word and the earth was born.

He lined the earth with whale-hide to secure it from the waters and shook it to make sure it was secure. This was the first earthquake, and all the earthquakes since that time are Taiko-mol retesting his work.

In the late Babylonian period there is a myth of the creation of cities in which the god Marduk is not only fecundator but mason, dam builder, and carpenter.

Marduk (II)

At one time, there were no reeds, no trees. No brick had been laid, no brick-mold built. All the lands were water. There were no houses, no temples for the gods, no cities, no living creatures. Marduk wanted to settle the gods in the dwelling of their hearts' delight so he built a reed frame over the waters and filled it with dirt he had created. He piled up a dam at the land's edge and turned a swamp into dry land.

The Lord Marduk created the Tigris and Euphrates and named them and set them on their course. He created grass, rushes in the marsh, woods, green plants of the field. He created orchards, forests, the cow and her young, the ewe and her young, the mountain goats. Together with the goddess Aruru he did these things, and then they created the seed of mankind.

Marduk built a brick-mold and laid bricks. He created the city of Nippur and its temple, Ekur. He created the city of Erech and its temple, Eanna. He built the city of Babylon and the city of Eridu and its temple, Esagila.

Lord Marduk did all these things long ago, and now we

recite these deeds when we come to purify the temple of the gods, the holy house.

It is, however, with the Abrahamic God of Judaism, Christianity, and Islam that the male image of God has achieved its greatest influence and power. This is the Creator God signified by the tetragrammaton, YHWH or JHVH (e.g., in the ninth-century B.C.E. text from Judah, which was reworked by the rabbis after the Babylonian Exile during the fourth and fifth centuries B.C.E. and which became Genesis 2:4–26). The letters are the four consonants of the name Jahwe, Yahweh, or Jehovah (the "self-existent"), too sacred to be spoken aloud. He was sometimes (e.g., in the eighth-century B.C.E. text reworked in the seventh century B.C.E. and again after the Babylonian captivity that became Genesis 1 and 2:1–4) referred to as Elohim (literally, the god, from the plural form of the Canaanite High God El—perhaps the actual god of Abraham) or Adonai (the lord). Christians and Muslims simply capitalize the generic word that is *god* in English, indicating the existence of only one god, whose name can be thought of as exactly that: for example, God in English, Dieu in French, Gott in German, Allah in Arabic. The fact that Jews, Christians, and Muslims share this God of Abraham, this monotheistic lord of the universe, is not to say that they have always agreed fully on his nature. The movement from Judaism to Christianity to Islam is part of the developing biography of God in the human mind since those ancient Stone Age days when he was associated with tricksterism and shamanism.

A consideration of the creation as revealed in the Hebrew Bible can tell us a great deal about God as Yahweh. It should be noted that Yahweh is often depicted as a stern and even ruthless storm and war god—the god who brought forth the devastating flood, the god who destroyed the enemies of his people. In much of the Old Testament, he is distinctly the exclusive god of the Hebrews who favors his chosen people above all others. It is he who, like the Babylonian Marduk before him, divides the waters to establish a new order, in this case by destroying the heathen hosts who chase his people after their release from Egypt. He is sometimes a jealous and even vain god. He tests Job mercilessly and allows Abraham to think he must sacrifice his only son Isaac to him. Yet in the creation story we discover a god whose concerns seem to be universal and benevolent. The world he creates is not the Hebrew world or the Yuki world or the Uitoto world; it is *the* world, which is why, however they might interpret it, Christians and Muslims could accept the Genesis story in essence.

Yahweh is an *ex nihilo* creator by the word (thus, "Let there be light"). Psalm 33:6,9 of the Bible tells us, "By the word of the lord were the heavens made; and all the host of them by the breath of his mouth. . . . For he spake, and it was done. . . ." And he is a *deus faber* creator. In Psalm 104:3, he is a builder who "layeth the beams of his chambers in the waters." And in the Book of Job (38:4–7) he reminds Job that is was he, Yahweh, who had "laid the foundations of the earth . . . laid the measures thereof . . . stretched the line upon it . . . laid the cornerstone thereof."

Yahweh

In the beginning God created the heaven and the earth. And the earth was without form, and void; and darkness was upon the face of the deep: and the Spirit of God moved upon the waters.

And God said, Let there be light: and there was light. And God saw the light, that it was good: and God divided the light from the darkness. And God called the light Day, and the darkness he called Night: and the evening and the morning were the first day.

And God said, Let there be a firmament in the midst of the waters: and let it divide the waters from the waters. And God made the firmament, and divided the waters which were under the firmament from the waters which were above the firmament: and it was so. And God called the firmament Heaven: and the evening and the morning were the second day.

And God said, Let the waters under the heaven be gathered together in one place, and let the dry land appear: and it was so. And God called the dry land Earth; and the gathering together of the waters he called Seas: and God saw that it was good. And God said, Let the earth bring forth grass, the herb yielding seed, and the fruit-tree yielding fruit after his kind, whose seed is in itself, upon the earth: and it was so. And the earth brought forth grass, and herb yielding seed after his kind, and the tree yielding fruit, whose seed was in itself, after his kind: and God saw that it was good. And the evening and the morning were the third day.

And God said, Let there be lights in the firmament of the heaven, to divide the day from the night; and let them be for signs, and for seasons, and for days, and years. And let them be for lights in the firmament of heaven to give light upon the earth: and it was so. And God made two great lights; the greater light to rule the day, and the lesser light to rule the night: he made the stars also. And God set them in the firmament of the heaven to give light upon the earth, and to rule over the day, and over the night, and to divide the light from the darkness: and God saw that it was good. And the evening and the morning were the fourth day.

And God said, Let the waters bring forth abundantly the moving creature that hath life, and fowl that may fly above the earth in the open firmament of heaven. And God created the great whales, and every living creature that moveth, and every winged fowl after his kind: and God saw that it was good. And God blessed them, saying, Be fruitful, and multiply, and fill the waters in the seas, and let fowl multiply in the earth. And the evening and the morning were the fifth day.

And God said, Let the earth bring forth the living creature after his kind, cattle, and the creeping thing, and beast of the earth after his kind: and it was so. And God made the beast of the earth after his kind, and cattle after their kind, and everything that creepeth upon the earth after his kind: and God saw that it was good.

God as architect of the universe: William Blake, *Europe,* plate 1, frontispiece, *The Ancient of Days* (ca. 1824). (Collection: Whitworth Art Gallery, University of Manchester)

And God said, Let us make man in our image, after our likeness: and let them have dominion over the fish of the sea, and the fowl of the air, and over the cattle, and over all the earth, and over every creeping thing that creepeth upon the earth. So God created man in his own image, in the image of God, he created him; male and female created he them. And God blessed them, and God said unto them, Be fruitful and multiply, and replenish the earth, and subdue it: and have dominion over the fish of the sea, and over the fowl of the air, and over every living thing that moveth upon the earth.

And God said, Behold, I have given you every herb bearing seed, which is upon the face of all the earth, and every tree, in which is the fruit of a tree yielding seed; to you it shall be meat. And to every beast of the earth, and to every fowl of the air, and to everything that creepeth upon the earth, wherein there is life, I have given every green herb for meat: and it was so. And God saw everything he had made: and behold, it was good. And the evening and the morning were the sixth day.

Thus the heavens and the earth were finished, and all the host of them. And on the seventh day God ended his work which he had made; and he rested on the seventh day from all his work which he had made. And God blessed the seventh day, and sanctified it; because that in it he had rested from all his work which God created and made.

(From King James Version, Genesis)

Although Christians have accepted the Genesis story as part of their religious heritage, the increase of non-Jewish—that is, gentile, and especially Greek—philosophy in the first century C.E. led to a new interpretation of that story. The beginning of the New Testament Gospel of John is, in effect, a Christian creation story that concentrates on the establishment of the divinity of Jesus as part of a triune god (Father, Son, and Holy Spirit) who is really no longer the Yahweh of the Old Testament. John's Word is at once the creative word of Yahweh in the Genesis creation and the ordering essence of God, which is incarnate in Jesus, but which was there as a part of God at the creation.

The Word

In the beginning was the Word, and the Word was with God, and the Word was God. The same was in the beginning with God. All things were made by him; and without him was not any thing made that was made. In him was life; and the life was the light of men. And the light shineth in the darkness; and the darkness comprehended it not.

There was a man sent from God, whose name was John. The same came for a witness, to bear witness of the Light, that all men might through him believe. He was not that Light, but was sent to bear witness of that Light. That was the true Light, which lighteth every man that cometh into the world. He was in the world, and the world was made by him, and the world knew him not. He came unto his own, and his own received him not. But as many as received him, to them gave he power to become the sons of God, even to them that believe on his name: which were born, not of blood, nor of the will of the flesh, nor of the will of man, but of God. And the Word was made flesh, and dwelt among us (and we beheld his glory, the glory as of the only begotten of the Father,) full of grace and truth.

John bare witness of him, and cried, saying, This was he of whom I spake, He that cometh after me, is preferred before me; for he was before me. And of his fulness have we all received, and grace for grace. For the law was given by Moses, but grace and truth came by Jesus Christ. No man hath seen God at any time; the only begotten Son, which is in the bosom of the Father, he hath declared him.

(From King James Version, John 1)

Although the Christian version of God has traditionally been masculine, following in the Hebrew tradition, it might well be argued—and often is—that God's masculinity, in spite of traditional depictions such as that of the white-bearded patriarch in the famous Blake painting, is not theologically significant. Indeed, there are those who would suggest that to attribute gender to God is to limit God to the reproductive cycle and thus to deny his immortality. In the somewhat mystical representation of God in John 1, we perhaps sense the beginning of a movement away from a patriarchal and masculine divinity to a more philosophical and even less personalized concept. For Christians, the personal aspect of God has more often than not been represented by the gentle and even, some would say, effeminate Jesus and popularly, if not theologically, by his increasingly deified mother. With the cult of Mary—immaculately conceived, assumed into heaven as Queen—Goddess, so absent from the world of Yahweh, begins to make her return. In contrast to Judaism, popular Christianity and to a great extent the church itself envision in the trinity and in the cult and doctrines of Mary, Queen of Heaven, at least the rudiments of a pantheon. In the idealized and often sentimentalized depictions of the Pietà—the mother and her dead son there are even inklings of a reemergence in the popular mind of the old Great Goddess–son-lover story. In the Christian concept of God—necessarily far less interesting as a personality than Jesus or Mary—a crack appears in the patriarchal vision of a monotheistic Supreme Being.

With the emergence of Islam in the seventh century C.E. the Abrahamic God, although referred to by the masculine pronoun, continues to lose his personal nature and to be perceived more as a divine creative power revealed in the world around us. And unlike in Christianity, there is no human figure to embody godhead. Allah's prophet, Muhammad, is explicitly denied divinity. The God of Islam is very much a mysterious being.

In the Koran, the sacred book of Allah, revealed to
Muhammad by the archangel Gabriel, the creation is again a
creation *ex nihilo* by the word.

Allah

It is Allah who gave you the earth and over it built Heaven,
and formed you and made you beautiful. He feeds you with
good things. This is Allah, your Lord. Blessed be Allah, the
Lord of the Worlds.

There is no god but Allah. Call upon him with pure worship. Praise be Allah, the Lord of the Worlds.

In six days Allah created the Heavens and the Earth, and
then mounted the throne. He throws the veil of night over the
day; he created the sun and the moon and the stars which go
by the laws he made. Is not the whole creation his? Blessed be
Allah, the Lord of the Worlds.

He it is who created you from dust, and the germs of life,
and of thick blood, and brought you into the world as infants.
Then he let you reach your full strength and grow old (though
some die before they are old). It is Allah who gives life and
death. He only needs to say "Be," and it is. Blessed be Allah,
the Lord of the Worlds.

The east and the west is Allah's, so whatever way you
turn, there is the face of Allah who is truly immense and
knows all. Blessed be Allah, the Lord of the Worlds.

Judaism, Christianity, and Islam, the "monotheistic" religions, have long been thought of by people in the Western
world as the highest form of religious expression. Yahweh,
God, and Allah were religious concepts, while Zeus and
Osiris, and even Siva and Visnu, were mere myths. Yet the
biography of God has revealed itself in sophisticated forms in

nearly every corner of the world. The process of depersonaliz-
ation and consequent degenderization we noted in the Christian and especially the Muslim God can be said to exist, as we
shall see, in more radical form in many of the religions of so-
called primitive peoples of Africa, the Americas, and the
South Pacific as well as in the "great religions" of Asia. There
is something in human nature that thirsts for a Supreme Being
who represents aspects of experience not characterized by
concepts such as conquest, hierarchy, or even justice.

VI

The Universalizing of The Archetype: God as Self and God Within

Yin–Yang symbol.

During the reign of the masculine sky-gods our picture of Supreme Being or ultimate reality has been deeply colored by the sense of God's transcendence. The high god, whether Zeus, Ra, Yahweh, God, or Allah, lives at a great distance from us—and must be approached through priestly intermediaries or a special mode of communication called prayer. In every sense, the sky-god is above us and beyond our experience. By contrast, Goddess of the Stone Age had been immanent in everything that was experience. The world itself was sacred with the presence of Goddess, who was in her earliest and purest form unpersonalized nature.

With the development of complex societies and hierarchies, divinities—goddesses and gods—took on more particular, humanlike personalities, and eventually we in the West—whether or not we are believers—have come to envision godhead in terms of a wise old king on a throne dispensing love, justice, compassion, or punishment to a somehow fallen human race.

But this picture is only one perspective or series of perspectives on the biography of God. There have always been peoples who have conceived of divinity as immanent, and as only metaphorically, if at all human like.

Before the emergence of Yahweh and the other versions of God as the Supreme Father, there had been many peoples—not only Goddess worshippers—who believed that the world they lived in was itself in some literal or metaphorical sense God. These people can in a very general sense be called animists, if by *animism* we mean a belief in the suffusion of inanimate objects by a god or gods. For the most part, the traditional monotheists have equated animism with paganism and polytheism as a primitive form of religion, clearly well below the level of forms such as Judaism, Christianity, and Islam. Even Shinto and Hinduism are sometimes belittled for their animistic aspects, and the animistic practices of certain Africans, Polynesians, and Native Americans have led proponents of the "higher religions" to see these people as distinctly inferior in terms of their religious understanding.

Yet a consideration of animistic myths reveals a sense of divinity that some would call advanced. Animists are spared, for instance, the personalized God and especially the monotheistic god, who must, the more specific his depiction, resemble particular groups more than others. As history shows, such a god is, more often than not, incoherent, a source of controversy rather than unity. The animistic deity, on the contrary, is everywhere; its mysterious presence—what the Japanese call *kami*, the Melanesian *mana*, or the Sioux Indians *wakan*—is felt primarily in the natural world, and the natural world belongs to all. It should be noted that gender is less important to the animistic god than to the more personalized gods. This is not to say that in the animistic myths there are not gods or goddesses. Depending on their cultural priorities, societies tend to give male or female gender to their gods, even if these gods are never seen, but are experienced only indirectly, in nature.

Perhaps the most dramatic examples of the male god in the animistic context occurs in creation myths in which the god literally becomes his creation. We have seen such an example in the Chinese myth of Phan Ku and in fact in all of the World Parent separation myths we considered in Section III, wherein the primal parents *are* the heavens and the earth.

In the creation myth of the Okanagan Indians of the Pacific Northwest, the creator himself does not become the world, but he makes the world out of a female being.

The Chief

The Chief created seven worlds. He made the earth and three worlds above it, and three worlds below it. This is what we believe now.

When the Chief made the earth, it was a female body that he stretched out with its head to the west. The west is the earth's head. You can see that all the rivers flow westward, and that is where heaven lies, the place we go when we die. Maybe we follow the rivers' courses.

So the earth was a woman most likely and the Chief stretched her out across the waters and transformed her into the earth we live on here. Then he made the Indians out of her flesh—balls of red earth or mud, which is why Indians are reddish in color. Then the chief made other races out of earth of other colors.

Eventually, these different races met and intermingled, so now there are many shades of color among people. But red earth is more closely akin to gold and copper than other kinds of soil, so Indians too are closer to gold. They are the finest of all the races.

Animism is particularly present in the myths of the South Pacific. This is the Tahitian story of how the god Ta'aroa created the world out of himself.

Ta'aroa

To begin with, there was only Ta'aroa, whose name means just that: Only. Unique.

Well, there was the shell, like that of an egg, in which Ta'aroa dwelled as it turned slowly, endlessly, in the great dark. But there was no sun, no moon, no land or mountain, no living things, no sea, no fresh water. But for Ta'aroa in his shell, and the continuous darkness, there was nothing.

At some time—nobody knows exactly when—Ta'aroa gave a sharp rap to the inside of his shell and it cracked open. Ta'aroa emerged into the dark and, standing on his shell, cried out.

"Is anybody up there? Is anyone below?" Receiving no answer, Ta'aroa began to get a bit annoyed. "Who is behind me? Who is in front?" Again, no answer—only his voice echoing in the void.

"Hey! You! Rock. Crawl over here!" he shouted, but there was no rock. "Hey, sand! Crawl over here!" But there was no sand. By now, confronting a world that was certainly disobedient if it existed at all, Ta'aroa was in high dudgeon.

In a rage, he grabbed part of his shell and threw it up to become the dome of the sky. Yet another part he made into rock and sand, but he was still angry. He wrenched out his spine and made a mountain range, his ribs the mountain slopes. He gouged out his vitals and threw them into the sky as clouds and turned his flesh into the warm weight of the earth. His arms and legs he installed to give the earth strength; his fingernails and toenails became the shells and scales of fishes; his feathers clothed the earth as trees, shrubs, and vines; his intestines became lobsters, shrimp, and eels in the rivers and seas; and his blood boiled up into a redness to adorn the sky and to organize rainbows.

Even so, Ta'aroa's head remained and, in fact, his body—though strewn about in his fit of creation—was indestructible. He was the master of all, and his creation grew.

In his head, Ta'aroa conjured up the gods, and later he conjured up mankind. And lying behind Ta'aroa's grand creation was the principle of the shell. Since Ta'aroa had a shell, so must everything else. The endless space where the gods placed the sun and the moon and the stars is a shell. The earth is the shell from which stones and water and plants spring. And both a man's and a woman's shell is a woman, for that is where they come into this world from.

Look around you. Everything has its shell.

There are, of course, animistic elements in many of the better-known mythologies. We have seen how the Babylonian High God Marduk made the world out of the slain monster-goddess Tiamat. And in myths of sacrifice, the Dying God becomes, in a sense, the essence of his world. Osiris becomes the grain; Dionysos, the grape; Jesus, the "bread of life."

In Hinduism, the god Visnu-Krishna reveals himself to the hero Arjuna in the *Bhagavad-Gita* as creation itself, and in another part of the *Mahabharata*, of which the *Bhagavad-Gita* is a part, he shows himself to the enemies of Arjuna as not only all of creation but as the essence of their own inner selves.

Krishna (II)

It is not known, of course, how this can happen but we do not ask questions about it for there are many things that we cannot be knowing. And what happened was that Krishna took on a form, a physical form, and appeared in the house of a man called Duryodhana. This Duryodhana was an angry man, a very bad man, and with his associate, Dushhasana, he was planning to make war upon his neighbors. His plan was to surprise them, never signaling his intentions, as is polite in these things.

Krishna, in his disguise, pled for peace and Duryodhana— in his paranoia—saw it as a plot. Against him.

Suddenly, everything was happening at once.

"It is a plot to kill me!" Duryodhana was shrieking. He called out to his colleague Dushhasana. "Grab him! Tie him up!" So Dushhasana is falling on Krishna and tying him up with ropes, while several old men who were present are protesting. They are aghast at the rudeness of this act: no decent society ever lays hands on an emissary. "Stop!" they are crying. "Both of you, stop!"

But then a miracle happens. Krishna—for an instant— reveals himself in his divine form. Suddenly everyone in the room is seeing him everywhere, in all things, even deep in their minds and their hearts. He is everywhere. And everything that is in him, the entire universe, the earth, the heavens and all creation, all this is visible for this instant.

Even the boorish Duryodhana sees it, sees Krishna *in* everyone there, even the lout Dushhasana. His senses reel like a
man who finds himself on a precipice.

"Is that you, Krishna?" he bellows. "I'm going to seize
you, tie you up. You'll be my prisoner and never interfere with
me again!" But he is dazed by the divinity of Krishna, his
everywhereness and nowhereness, and gives up in despair.

And, in a cloud of smoke, Krishna disappears.

In Tantrism, a mystical outgrowth of Hinduism and Bud-
dhism, the animistic image of Visnu as the universe serves as a
point of meditation suggesting that in a sense we are god and
the universe is within us.

The sense of God as Self and God within is perhaps most
fully revealed in the Hindu concept of Brahman. Brahman as
Atman (Self) is within all that is but is, as Brahman, beyond
not only personhood but definable being; Brahman is the first
cause—the life force—the power behind ritual and sacred
words. He is the Om, the Word, in Western terms *logos*. Brahman is everywhere and nowhere, and everything that is—
including the goddesses and great gods themselves, even Siva
and Visnu-Krishna—is Brahman. Theologians caution us not
to confuse Brahman, a philosophical concept, with God, the
ultimate being. But mythologically speaking, Brahman is, in
fact, a logical outgrowth of both animism and monotheism.
Brahman avoids the traps of gender, culture, and history.
Brahman is the essence within and without. Brahman is neither male nor female, although the male pronoun is sometimes
applied to him, and he can take form in the gods of the Hindu
trinity: Siva the yogic-destroyer, Visnu the preserver, and
Brahma the creator—*Brahma* being the masculine form of the
neuter *Brahman*. Brahman is ineffable and unknowable, beyond our comprehension, and yet Brahman is our reason for
being. In terms of our biographical approach to God, Brahman
is the most accurate picture we can hope to paint of the essence of God, as opposed to particularized culture expressions

Om.

of God. As such, Brahman can be said to be the power behind
God's many cultural masks, whether Zeus, Osiris, Goddess,
or the great Abrahamic God himself.

In the *Upanishads* (ca. 800–600 B.C.E.), we read the following exchange.

Brahman

USHASTA CAKRAYANA: Yajnavalkya, tell me. Explain the
    Brahman who is present at all times and directly seen,
    the Brahman who is the self in all things.

YAJNAVALKYA: This is your self. Your self is within every
    thing.

U.C.: *Which* is in *all* things, Yajnavalkya?

Y.:   He who is breathing in while you are breathing in—that
    is the self of you which is in all things. He who is breath-
    ing out while you are breathing out—that is the self of
    you that is in all things. He who breathes up with you,
    he who breathes down with you—that is your self that is
    in all things. He is your self that is in all things.

U.C. (sighing): You are explaining this to me much the way
    one might say "This is a cow," "This is a horse." Now,
    please, explain to me the *Brahman* who is directly seen,
    this self that is within all things.

Y.:   You cannot see the seer of all things. You cannot hear
       the hearer of hearing. You cannot think the thinker of
       thinking. You cannot understand the understander of
       understanding. He is yourself, which is in all things.
              Everything else is of evil.

In China, the Tao, like Brahman, is a concept. But for our
purposes it can also be seen as ultimate reality or God. Like
Brahman, it is everywhere and nowhere, the essence of all that
is. Without it there can be no order; it is *logos*. In the *Tao Te
Ching*, the legendary Lao-tzu writes about the Tao.

The Tao (I)

The Tao, the Way, is like an empty vessel; it can be drawn
from without ever needing to be filled. It is bottomless. It is
the maker of everything in the world.

      In it, sharpness becomes blunt, tangles unravel, glare is
tempered, and the noise of the days is soothed. It is like a
deep pool that never dries up.

      We cannot tell if it was the child of something else but
surely, as an image without substance, it existed before the
creation.

      The great Tao drifts like a boat, going this way and that.
All creatures owe their existence to it but it never disowns
them. It covers everything and everyone but never claims to
be the master of anything. You can call it *lowly*.

      All creatures obey it without knowing that it is their mas-
ter, so you can call it *great*.

      Just so, the sage never makes a show of greatness and, in
doing so, achieves greatness.

Like Brahman, the Tao is beyond gender. It can be male or
female or neither. In connection with the Tao within, Lao-
tzu sees it in its female form, almost as a version of Goddess.

The Tao (II)

What began all things under heaven we can speak of as the
mother of everything. And he who apprehends the mother—
the Tao, the Way— knows the sons as well—the universe and
all things in it.

He who knows the sons will cling all the more closely to
the mother and never suffer harm till the end of his days.

Just as good sight means seeing the very small, strength
means holding on to the weak, the Way, the Tao.

So he who has used the outer-light, he who has known the
sons, can return to the inner-light of self-knowledge and be
safe from harm.

This is called resorting to the always-so.

The perfect icon for the Tao is the Yin–Yang, in which opposites join and express each other within themselves (see illus-
tration at beginning of chapter).

The search for God as Self—God within—has been pursued consistently by people we call mystics. Mystics have
existed even in the great patriarchal monotheistic religions
and have stressed the possibility of achieving union with ultimate reality, which they tend to see as an all-encompassing
mystery existing within each individual rather than as a single,
necessarily limiting personalized being isolated in heaven.
"The goal of the true Buddhist," says the Zen master, "is to
be rid of the Buddha," that is, to move beyond the personalized icon to the Great Mystery within. Prayer, the sacred
language, in this context becomes meditation rather than a

personalized petitioning of a powerful overlord. The sacred
texts and rituals become aids to the process of breaking down
barriers between the god within and the typically overoc-
cupied, unfocused individual. In a sense, these disciplines
resemble those ancient shaman journeys in which the shaman
communes with the spirit world. In yoga or the dervish dance
or deep meditation, we become the shaman, the trickster who
breaks the barrier between the two worlds.

Mysticism in Judaism has taken several forms, the most
interesting of which is the discipline called the Kabbalah.
Influenced by the mystics of the Islamic world, the Kabbalists
emphasize a form of God within called En Sof, which is also
somewhat like the Hindu Atman. En Sof is a being beyond
personality who gradually reveals the mysteries of himself and
of creation to those who open themselves to him. In the *Zohar*,
a thirteenth-century work by the Spanish Kabbalist Moses de
León, we find a creation myth involving the self-revelation of
En Sof.

En Sof

At the beginning, a dark flame emerged from the innermost
recesses of En Sof. It was neither black nor white, red nor
green, but colorless, formless. It was the highest divinity because it was *nothing*—this flame. Being nothing, it was unlike
anything else that exists. It can also be thought of as the
Supreme Crown of Divinity, the womb of nothingness from
which everything would arise.

Then En Sof further expressed itself. The flame grew,
and bright colors radiated from it, lighting everything below
that had been hidden in the secret mysteries of En Sof. It was
the Beginning—*Bereshit*, which is the first word of creation.
This was the point in En Sof's self-revelation called Wisdom,
the ideal form of all created things. Beyond Wisdom lay Intel-
ligence and that is as far as humans can penetrate. No one
knows who En Sof is, though it has revealed itself to some
degree to the limited range of human comprehension. The

closer we come to understanding En Sof, the deeper in dark mystery En Sof becomes.

Christians, too, have had their mystics. The thirteenth-century German mystics Meister Eckhart and Gertrude the Great, Dame Julian of Norwich in the fourteenth century, and the sixteenth-century Spanish writers Saints Teresa of Avila and John of the Cross all spoke of knowing the God within.

The most highly developed mystical system among the Abrahamic religions is that of the Sufis of Islam. There are many sects of Sufis or dervishes.

The best-known Sufi is the Persian Jalal al-Din Rumi, the thirteenth-century founder of the Whirling Dervishes in Konya, in what is now Turkey. Like most Sufis, Rumi was opposed to extreme sectarianism. He spoke, for example, of the Christian story of the virgin birth of Jesus as an appropriate symbol for the birth of the Self in the soul of the mystic. Rumi accepted Islam as his particular vehicle of faith but did not believe that his religion possessed the only path to truth. In the collection of Rumi's poems called the *Masnawi*, he tells this tale of God and Moses.

Rumi's God

Once Moses overheard a shepherd talking. It sounded as if the shepherd were talking to an uncle or a friend, but he was talking to God.

"I would like to help you wherever you are, wash your clothes, pick lice from you, kiss your hands and feet at bedtime. All I can say, recalling you, is *ahhhhhhhhhhhhh* and *ayyyyyyyyy*,"

Moses was very upset. "Are you talking in such a way to the very creator of heaven and earth? Don't you have more respect?"

The shepherd hung his head and wandered off, saddened.
But God came to rebuke Moses, saying:

What's wrong for you is right for him.
Your poison can be another's honey.
I don't care about purity or diligence in worship.
Or impurity and sloth.
They mean nothing to me. I am above all that.
One way of worshipping is as good as another.

Hindus do Hindu things.
Muslims in India do what they do.
It is all praise, and it is all right.

I don't listen to the words worshippers say.
I look inside for humility. That's reality.
Mere language, phraseology, isn't reality.
I want burning, burning!

Be friends, all of you, with your burning.
Burn your thinking in humility.
Burn your phrases.

For Rumi, the goal of the mystic, whether Jewish, Islamic,
Christian, or Hindu, was to transcend the artificial barriers
established by orthodoxies between the individual and the
God within.

In Akshehir, a town near Konya, is the tombstone of the
purely legendary trickster–wise fool, Nassredin Hodja, whose
bizarre escapades were frequently used by the Sufis to illustrate their philosophy. As one approaches the grave, one no-
tices a gate with an absurdly large padlock maintaining the
security of the Islamic turban-topped tombstone behind it.
Upon closer inspection, two details stand out. First, it becomes clear that the gate stands alone, that there is no contin-
uation of fencing from either side of it. To come close to the
tomb, the visitor need only walk around the forbidding gate.
Second, there is a small hole in the tombstone itself—

presumably a peephole out of which the Hodja can look to see who has stopped at the gate and who has had the sense to see that the gate is no barrier to the mystery within.

In the dance tradition established by Rumi, his followers—dressed in flowing gowns and tall cylindrical hats—whirl gracefully around a stationary figure. They do so sometimes for hours, breaking through the boundaries of ordinary gravity and dizziness to achieve the ecstasy that is the experience of God.

Various other disciplines intended to open the individual to union with the god within have been devised over the centuries. Meditation on sacred objects, fasting, yogic exercises, and dancing are all such disciplines. In contemporary times, the mystics have similarities with the students of psychology who find the god within a useful metaphor for the idea of the Self buried in the depths of the unconscious world, what Jung called the "maternal" depths.

Scientific inquiry, indeed, is not generally taken as a means of exploring theological matters, or even matters that have a moral dimension. Scientists seek the ways nature *works*, not why it works. Yet astrophysicists and astronomers, armed with mathematics and other unimaginably powerful tools, do look back into the origin of things, the beginning of the universe. In the origins of this universe and in the death of stars that collapse into what are called black holes, some see the possibility of many other universes existing on what seem unimaginable planes—universes of energy and matter finally collapsing into infinitesimally small places called singularities and, possibly, vanishing only to emerge outside into another place of creation—another universe aborning. There is plenty of disagreement—the astrophysicists' tools are not omnipotent—but most agree on a general story of how this universe began.

The Big Bang

There is a singularity somewhere. It is infinitely small, and infinitely heavy, infinitely dense. It contains all the matter and energy a universe would require. And then, perhaps of its own accord, it explodes in a violent seizure too great to imagine, though some have tried to quantify it into whatever form of things existed before matter and energy, before dimension and time.

At any rate, it exploded, and in such tiny fractions of seconds that they can only be spoken of but never comprehended, the universe began to inflate, to grow, to change, to fall into an orderly evolution of elements and existence. It followed the rules which some mathematicians can nearly divine, becoming stars, galaxies, gases, things, continents, life, parrots, music, fastfood stores. It became temples, and weapons, and the human imagination, and every living and extinct creature that has ever dwelled here on the planet earth—itself a remote backwater in the exurbs of an unimportant galaxy in an unmeasured universe.

Or, perhaps, it is the most important corner of the universe, this earth—and for reasons we cannot ever fathom.

Certainly astrophysicists will never fathom the reasons, if they exist but they can and do, from time to time, wonder what lay before that Big Bang.

Before?

Nothing, for in it time, too, was created.

Well, then, *beyond* it somehow.

There are physicists who speculate that beyond or outside of the Big Bang there was what you might think of as an urge—an urge for some kind of creation and order, possibly a mathematical urge.

Which, of course, should sound familiar by now.

However we envision divinity in the years and centuries to come, it seems likely that except among so-called fundamentalists, who would stop at the Hodja's gate and look no further, the trend in the biography of God is toward a reunion with that of Goddess. The logical end result would seem to be a genderless divinity who bears more resemblance to the animistic Goddess of the Paleolithic caves, to Brahman, and to the God within of the mystics than to the Great Goddess of Çatal Hüyük or the Great God of Abraham. As Supreme Being becomes less Goddess and less God, it speaks more clearly to the essential human need for unity and understanding. In the androgynous life force within us and around us, we discover the lost Self that can be the source of our being.

Selected Bibliography

Abrahams, Roger D. *African Folktales: Traditional Stories of the Black World*. New York, 1983.

Armstrong, Karen. *A History of God*. New York, 1993.

Aron, Robert. *The God of the Beginnings*. New York, 1966.

Ballou, Robert O., ed. *The Bible of the World*. New York, 1939.

Baring, Anne, and Jules Cashford. *The Myth of the Goddess: Evolution of an Image*. New York, 1991.

Beier, Ulli. *The Origin of Life and Death: African Creation Myths*. London, 1966.

The Bhagavadgita. Translated by R. C. Zaehner. Oxford, 1969.

Biallas, Leonard J. *Myths: Gods, Heroes, and Saviors*. Mystic, Conn., 1986.

Bierhorst, John. *The Mythology of North America*. New York, 1985.

Boer, Charles, trans. *The Homeric Hymns*. Chicago, 1970.

Bolen, Jean Shinoda. *Gods in Everyman: A New Psychology of Men's Lives and Loves*. New York, 1989.

Brandon, S. G. F. *Creation Legends of the Ancient Near East*. London, 1963.

Campbell, Joseph. *The Masks of God: Creative Mythology*. New York, 1968.

Campbell, Joseph. *The Masks of God: Occidental Mythology*. New York, 1964.

Campbell, Joseph. *The Masks of God: Oriental Mythology*. New York, 1962.

Campbell, Joseph. *The Masks of God: Primitive Mythology*. New York, 1959.

Campbell, Joseph. *The Mythic Image*. Princeton, 1983.

Campbell, Joseph. *The Power of Myth*. New York, 1988.

Campbell, Joseph. *The Way of the Animal Powers*. London, 1983.

Clark, R. T. Rundle. *Myth and Symbol in Ancient Egypt*. London, 1959.

Colum, Padraic. *Myths of the World*. 1930. New York, 1972. Originally published as *Orpheus*.

Crossley-Holland, Kevin. *The Norse Myths*. New York, 1980.

Davidson, H. R. Ellis. *Gods and Myths of Northern Europe*. Baltimore, 1964.

Dodson Gray, Elizabeth. *Patriarchy as a Conceptual Trap*. Wellesley, Mass., 1982.

Dumezil, Georges. *Mitra-Varuna: An Essay on Two Indo-European Representations of Sovereignty*. New York, 1988.

Eisler, Raine. *The Chalice and the Blade: Our History, Our Future*. San Francisco, 1987.

Eliade, Mircea. *Essential Sacred Writings from Around the World*. 1967. San Francisco, 1992. Originally published as *From Primitives to Zen*.

Eliade, Mircea. *A History of Religious Ideas*. Vol. 1, *From the Stone Age to the Eleusinian Mysteries*. Translated by William Trask. Chicago, 1979.

Eliade, Mircea. *A History of Religious Ideas*. Vol. 2, *From Gautama Buddha to the Triumph of Christianity*. Translated by William Trask. Chicago, 1984.

Eliade, Mircea. *Patterns in Comparative Religion*. 1958. New York, 1974.

Eliade, Mircea. *Shamanism: Archaic Techniques of Ecstasy*. Translated by William Trask. 1964. Princeton, 1972.

Eliade, Mircea, ed. *The Encyclopedia of Religion*. 16 vols. New York, 1987.

Erdoes, Richard, and Alfonso Ortiz. *American Indian Myths and Legends*. New York, 1984.

Frazer, Sir James. *The New Golden Bough*. Edited by Theodor Gaster. New York, 1959.

Freund, Philip. *Myths of Creation*. New York, 1965.

Gadon, Elinor W., *The Once and Future Goddess*. San Francisco, 1989.

Gates, Henry Louis, Jr. *The Signifying Monkey: A Theory of African-American Literary Criticism*. New York, 1988.

Gimbutas, Marija. *The Goddesses and Gods of Old Europe, 7000–3500 B.C.: Myths, Legends and Cult Images*. London, 1982.

Gimbutas, Marija. *The Language of the Goddess*. San Francisco, 1989.

Graves, Robert. *The Greek Myths*. 2 vols. Baltimore, 1955.

Guthrie, Stewart Elliott. *Faces in the Clouds: A New Theory of Religion*. New York, 1993.

Guthrie, W. K. C. *The Greeks and Their Gods*. Boston, 1950.

Hart, George. *Egyptian Gods and Goddesses*. New York, 1986.

Hesiod. *Theogony*. Translated by Dorothea Wender. Harmondsworth, 1973.

Holy Bible, King James Version.

Hooke, S. H. *Middle Eastern Mythology*. Harmondsworth, 1963.

Jung, Carl G. *Four Archetypes: Mother, Rebirth, Spirit, Trickster*. Translated by R. F. C. Hull. 1959. Princeton, 1969.

Jung, Carl G., and Carl Kerenyi. *Essays on a Science of Mythology: The Myth of the Divine Child and the Mysteries of Eleusis*. Translated by R. F. C. Hull. 1949. Princeton, 1969.

Kramer, Samuel Noah. *From the Poetry of Sumer*. Berkeley, 1979.

Kramer, Samuel Noah. *History Begins at Sumer*. London, 1958.

Kramer, Samuel Noah. *Mythologies of the Ancient World*. Garden City, N.Y., 1961.

Kramer, Samuel Noah. *Summerian Mythology*. New York, 1961.

Kramer, Samuel Noah, and John Maier. *Myths of Enki, the Crafty God*. New York, 1989.

Leeming, David A. *Flights: Readings in Magic, Mysticism, Fantasy, and Myth*. New York, 1974.

Leeming, David A. *Mythology*. New York, 1976.

Leeming, David A. *Mythology: The Voyage of the Hero*. New York, 1981.

Leeming, David A. *The World of Myth*. New York, 1990.

Leeming, David A., and Margaret A. Leeming. *Encyclopedia of Creation Myths*. Santa Barbara, Calif., 1994

Leeming, David A., and Jake Page. *Goddess: Myths of the Female Divine*. New York, 1994.

Lerner, Gerda. *The Creation of Patriarchy*. New York, 1986.

Levy, G. Rachel. *Religious Conceptions of the Stone Age, and Their Influence upon European Thought*. 1948. New York, 1963.

Long, Charles H. *Alpha: The Myths of Creation*. New York, 1963.

Maclagan, David. *Creation Myths: Man's Introduction to the World*. London, 1977.

Marshack, Alexander. *The Roots of Civilization*. New York, 1972.

Mascaro, Juan, trans. *The Upanishads*. Baltimore, 1965.

Mellaart, James. *Çatal Hüyük: A Neolithic Town in Anatolia*. New York, 1967.

Mellaart, James. *Earliest Civilizations of the Near East*. London, 1967.

Nilsson, Martin P. *A History of Greek Religion*. New York, 1964.

O'Flaherty, Wendy Doniger. *Hindu Myths: A Sourcebook Translated from the Sanskrit*. New York, 1975.

Olcott, William Tyler. *Myths of the Sun*. New York, 1914.

Otto, Walter F. *The Homeric Gods: The Spiritual Significance of Greek Religion*. Translated by Moses Hadas. London, 1954.

Ovid. *Metamorphosis*. Translated by Mary M. Innes. Harmondsworth, 1955.

Perry, John Weir. *Lord of the Four Quartets: The Mythology of Kingship*. New York, 1966.

Pettazzoni, Raffaele. *The All-Knowing God: Researches into Religion and Culture*. Translated by H. J. Rose. London, 1956.

Popol Vuh: The Sacred Book of the Ancient Quiche Maya. Translated by Delia Goetz and Sylvanus G. Morley from the translation of Adrian Recinos. Norman, Okla., 1950.

Puhvel, Jaan. *Comparative Mythology*. Baltimore, 1987.

Racz, Istvan. *The Unknown God*. New York, 1970.

Radin, Paul. *Monotheism Among Primitive Peoples*. London, 1924.

Radin, Paul. *The Trickster: A Study in American Indian Mythology*. New York, 1956.

Rao, Shanta Rameshwar, trans. *The Mahabharata* (abridged). New Delhi. 1974.

Rosenberg, Donna. *World Mythology*. Lincoln Woods, Ill., 1989.

Shah, Indries. *The Sufis*. New York, 1964.

Singer, June. *Androgyny: Toward a New Theory of Sexuality*. New York, 1976.

Smart, Ninian. *The Long Search*. Boston, 1977.

Smith, Mark S. *The Early History of God: Yahweh and the Other Deities in Ancient Israel*. San Francisco, 1990.

Sproul, Barbara C. *Primal Myths: Creation Myths Around the World*. New York, 1979.

Sturluson, Snorri. *The Prose Edda: Tales from Norse Mythology*. Translated by Jean I. Young. 1954. Berkeley, 1973.

Thompson, William Irwin. *The Time Falling Bodies Take to Light: Mythology, Sexuality, and the Origin of Culture*. New York, 1981.

Tyler, Hamilton A. *Pueblo Gods and Myths*. Norman, Okla., 1964.

Tylor, Edward B. *Primitive Culture*. 1871. New York, 1960.

Weigle, Mary. *Creation and Procreation*. Philadelphia, 1989.

Wolkstein, Diane, and Samuel Noah Kramer. *Inanna, Queen of Heaven and Earth: Her Stories and Hymns from Sumer*. London, 1983.

Zimmer, Heinrich. *Myths and Symbols in Indian Art and Civilization*. 1946. Princeton, 1972.

Index

Page numbers in italics refer to illustrations.